STOP PAINFUL PARENTING

TALES FROM OUR SIDE OF THE MAT

Paul Prendergast and Carol Davis, LCSW

ISBN: 978-1-4834-6397-1 (sc)
ISBN: 978-1-4834-6396-4 (e)

Lulu Publishing Services rev. date: 01/27/2017

To Dawn Prendergast—thank you for letting me ride your coattails

CONTENTS

Preface.. ix

Foreword..xiii

Acknowledgments xv

Chapter 1 Perseverance... 1

Chapter 2 Integrity... 10

Chapter 3 Honesty 38

Chapter 4 Respect 70

Chapter 5 Self-Control 92

Chapter 6 Courtesy 105

Chapter 7 Six Degrees of Awesome 110

About the Author..115

PREFACE

I've been teaching the martial arts for more than thirty-five years. I have owned a karate school for more than twenty-six years. Thousands of children and parents have crossed my path, and I'm outraged. I'm tired of the weak methods parents instill in their children. I'm tired of the nonsense. I'm tired of the lack of parental guidance and example. Throughout the years, I've witnessed successful parents and families and unsuccessful parents and families. The successful parents all have one common denominator: setting a good example.

When I opened my first karate school twenty-six years ago, I would never have thought I would deal with parents who grew marijuana, had fistfights in my lobby, or cheated on their spouses. I never thought I'd deal with a mom so drunk she pissed her pants while waiting to pick up her child or a boy who drew pictures with his own poo on the walls of my bathroom. My instructor never taught me how to defend myself against these types of attackers.

I hope this book will teach people to be more conscious of their words and actions in the presence of their children and other people's children. These children will become parents, guardians, coaches, teachers, and mentors. These children will become aware how important their role is. When I first started writing this book, I was conflicted about sharing these stories.

I was hesitant about who might get offended, who might object to my profanity at times, and who would be put off by it. Isn't that the problem today? We are all so worried about being politically correct and filtering our words and actions. Have we forgotten about right and wrong? How are we helping our children by insulating them from correction? We all want to be our children's buddies. We have forgotten that parents are the example. We are blueprints and models for them.

At times, I doubted myself. Do I have the experience and/ or education to write about parenting? I do. I think teaching and mentoring thousands of families and their children for more than thirty years qualifies me. Being a single father who is raising a daughter alone qualifies me. I am blessed with a daughter who makes me proud every single day by being kind, generous, and compassionate with others while reaching the dean's list in her first four semesters at college. These things qualify me. I am not a perfect parent. I'm just like everyone else. I'm doing the best I can, but I learn from my mistakes. I have learned a lot from watching other parents.

This book shares the stories of parents who have struggled with raising children. If we don't examine our motives as parents, we may influence our children in ways that are not helpful. In this book, I share stories of parents who haven't had the opportunity to look at themselves and the impact it has on their children. I have changed everyone's name to protect his or her privacy.

Imagine that I'm holding a large mirror on my side of my body. I want parents to see what the rest of us are seeing. As a psychotherapist, Carol Davis, LCSW, has worked with individuals and families for more than thirty-five years. Carol offers clinical wisdom to help them overcome shortcomings and provide hope for our children. Whatever our issues are as parents, we are presented with the challenge to improve our children's lives. I invite you to read these stories with an open heart; there might be more going on in these homes than we know about.

We are fortunate to live in a time when we can be more present in our children's lives. We can learn how to be even more present. I hope this book will teach parents new ways to shine for our children. All parents are not painful parents. This book shares stories of "painful parenting," and those parents need to take a good, hard look at themselves. When reading this book, keep in mind that we don't want to repeat our mistakes or shortcomings. We don't want to pass on our crap to our children. Whatever our flaws are as parents, we must fix them, hide them, or change them!

No one thinks they are bad parents when they are parenting. If hindsight is twenty-twenty, let this book be your corrective lens for parenting. Your children are counting on your clarity now. Your clarity counts now. You and your children will suffer greatly if you wait to see what you could have done better.

Let us be more present. Let us be shining examples to our children of what is right. When our children think of honesty, integrity, courtesy, respect, and indomitable spirit, they should think of their parents.

FOREWORD

Four years ago, I walked into Paul Prendergast Karate with my five-year-old son. He was eager to try the martial arts, which he had deemed "cool," and I entered the school with a mixture of hope and anxiety. At times, my son had difficulty reining in his impulsivity, and I knew that self-control was one of the cornerstones of karate. I was willing to give it a go since traditional team sports had not worked out for my little guy. I desperately wanted him to have an outlet for his never-ending abundance of energy.

I could have left the anxiety at home and simply channeled the hope.

The first few years were often challenging for my son. There were times when he lost focus or needed to be redirected to the task at hand. The instructors had all worked with special-needs kids before, and they handled his impetuous nature with grace and patience. With consistency and more than a dash of discipline, my boy performs his moves with eagerness, willingly practices at home, and strives for excellence when he's on the mat.

This turnaround would never have happened without the comprehensive program at PPK.

At PPK, Master Paul Prendergast has built a school that focuses on executing karate moves with excellence and emphasizes character development. The students are reminded frequently to behave for their parents, treat their siblings with respect, and try their best in school. There are opportunities for leadership within the program and chances for charitable contributions to families inside and outside the PPK family. Students are asked to strive for their personal best in all domains, and the instructors lead by example. Most kids and families rise to the challenges set forth for them.

Unfortunately, a few do not. Subsequently, Master Paul has

chosen to share these families' stories with you in this book. He hopes that all families who read his words will ultimately choose to strive for their own version of excellence.

I've had the honor of editing his manuscript, and I've been shocked by the events that have transpired within the school and impressed by the maturity with which they were handled. In each chapter, Master Paul tells the tale of families who do not adhere to the discipline recommended by the principles of PPK. He suggests alternative choices for each family. These choices are sanctioned by a practicing psychotherapist who imparts her wisdom at the end of every chapter.

This compelling saga and cautionary tale is worth reading. Master Paul is no stranger to adversity. He had to overcome many struggles in childhood and lost his beloved wife far too young. His writing comes from a place of compassion. No matter what challenges readers face, there is always a choice to be made about how to handle them: with defeat or grace. Master Paul has consistently chosen the latter.

It is his hope that after reading his memoir you will too.
—Kimberlee Rutan McCafferty, author of Raising Autism: Surviving the Early Years

ACKNOWLEDGMENTS

Stop Painful Parenting: Tales from Our Side of the Mat has taken more than a year to write, compile, and edit. One of the greatest joys in creating this book has been working with people who gave the project their time and attention. We would like to thank the following people for their support and friendship. Without them, this book could never have been created.

To my love, Colleen Leonard: Your love, support, dedication, friendship, and beautiful smile are my strength. Thank you for loving me.

To Peaches: I am everything I am today because you loved me.

To my daughter, Shea Prendergast, my pride and joy: You make me proud every day. Thanks for being the best daughter a father could have.

To my sister Noreen Miller: Thanks for all you do. You are always there. You are always a team player. Love you, Neen.

To my writing partner, Carol Davis: Thank you for your patience and wisdom—and mostly for your friendship.

To my managers at PPK, David Zaffos and Andrew Andreadis: You are my left and right arms. Words don't do justice to what you boys mean to me. Thank you for your dedication and support.

To the staff at PPK: You guys and girls rock! Thank you for being the "product of the product."

To Kimberlee Rutan McCafferty: Thank you for your friendship and patience during the early phases of editing. Your thoughts and insights were a huge help.

To my brothers in the martial arts, Professor Tom Curry and Master Dusty Everson: Thank you for many wonderful years of friendship, morning motivational calls, and breakfast mastermind sessions.

To Grand Master Art Beins: Thank you, sir, for sharing this

extraordinary gift with me thirty-six years ago. I humbly bow to you, sir.

To Mario Hundertajlo: Thank you for your inspiration and for sharing your ideas with me.

To my friend Janet Tauro: Thank you for your support and time. You are one of the most caring and generous people I know.

To Sean V. Bradley: Thank you, sir, for the gift of your time. It was very valuable and appreciated. Your enthusiasm and work ethic inspire me.

To my sisters Ellen and Nancy and Gary: You have supported this project with love and support.

To Paul Prendergast, my writing partner: Thank you for encouraging me to write this book.

To Larry Thompson: Thank you for your time, energy, and positive encouragement.

To Larry Bailin: Thank you for your wisdom, friendship, and example.

1

Perseverance

It's hard to beat a person who never gives up.
—Babe Ruth

My Daughter's Touch

I 've been asked why I would start a book about parenting with a story like the one you are about to read. It's simple: I hope this story inspires others. I hope it directs parents to focus on their children and the big picture more than the little distractions of life that take us off our targets. We want to raise happy, healthy, confident children who strive for progress and improvement and are loaded with self-esteem. No matter what life throws at us, we must not falter. We must not fail our children.

This is my story.

If not for my daughter's hand upon my shoulder, I would be in jail. Her simple, soft touch, which only a daughter or a mother could apply so convincingly, saved a policeman's life—and my life as well.

The martial arts is a misnomer. We learn and train for combat and self-defense and to be able to protect ourselves quickly and easily should we be given the cause. In karate, we train to perfect our character. The chief purpose is to "perfect one's character" and be better than we are. We seek perfection of character from the inside out, which is something we should do in every moment of every day of our lives.

We practice fighting so we do not have to fight. That night, I wanted to fight. I wanted to fight hard, kill, hurt, and maim.

Dawn and I loved the weekends and spending time with friends. One Saturday night, no one wanted to hang out with us. Since everybody had plans, we just enjoyed each other's company. Our big night out after a long week was TGI Friday's. What can I say? I'm a sport. Dawn loved their pecan-crusted chicken salad, and that's where we went.

Earlier that day, Dawn had been feeling productive and decided to clean and organize our office in the back of the house. I had files, books, and computers everywhere. It looked like a bomb had gone off in there, but she was on a mission. She was going to organize the office.

After our meal, we headed home. It was a short night, but it was fun. I always laughed with her. I immediately crashed on the couch and flicked on the TV like all men who had just gobbled down a dry pecan-crusted salad from Friday's. Dawn headed upstairs to soak in a hot tub, which was her routine.

After a good soak in the tub, Dawn came downstairs. She was wearing her beloved muumuu. She must have gotten some more energy because she was on the go again. The office situation was eating at her. Dawn went back to survey the office, came back out, and said, "You've got shit everywhere."

I agreed and told her I would be right there.

"No, stay there on the couch. You'll be in the way," she said. Moments later she called my name like I had never heard before. It was a faint and labored tone, and it didn't even sound like her voice.

I answered her like most guys who are watching TV. "What?"

"Get in here!" she cried.

It was not the cry of someone who was pissed at me for leaving my crap all over a small office in the back of the house. I hustled to see what was wrong and found her on her knees. Her face was white, she was in pain, she had trouble speaking, and her breathing was shallow.

She could barely talk. I was cautious at first because Dawn was a trickster. She would think nothing about pretending to be sick or injured before scaring me. That was her sense of humor. I hesitated for a few seconds, but when I placed my hand on her shoulder to ask if she was okay, she pushed me away. The pain was too much with my big hand on her shoulder.

I called 911. As I was speaking to the operator, Dawn moved from her knees to her back. She was leaving me. I yelled, "Dawn, stay with me."

The operator told me to help her sit upright. I juggled the phone from one ear to the other and tried to sit her up with my free arm. I had ruptured my bicep tendon and had surgery to repair it eight weeks earlier, and holding the phone and Dawn at the same time was very difficult.

The operator told me to keep her awake and put an aspirin under her tongue. We both thought she was having a heart attack. I hung up with the operator because I could no longer do both things at the same time. As my beloved slumped in the chair, she was getting paler. Her lips were turning blue, and it was difficult for her to talk. I had been trained in CPR for years, and I knew it was not good.

For years, Dawn had dealt with high blood pressure, so I thought she was having a stroke. Her speech was slurring. I asked her what day it was.

"Thursday" she answered. It was Saturday.

I asked her to smile for me. She tried, but only half her face would engage. I started to cry. The woman known for her beauty, spirit, and incredible smile could not smile.

As my daughter watched, I yelled for her to gather any pills and prescriptions with Mommy's name on it. I knew were going to the hospital. "I need underwear," she said. She repeated as best she could and as often as she could.

Anytime I asked her where the pain was, she would say, "Get me my undies" Who knew those would be her last words to me. She didn't want anyone to see her in just her muumuu.

Her color was bad. Dawn's body was slumped in the chair, and she stopped asking me for her undies. I begged her to stop. I yelled, "Don't do this to me!" She was dying, and I yelled at her. I will regret it for the rest of my life. I could see very little life in her. The woman who embodied the word "life" was losing hers.

I moved her to the floor, and my CPR education started to kick in. I checked for breathing sounds, and they were there, but they were weak. She still had a heartbeat. I could do nothing at that point. No compressions, no breaths, nothing.

As I turned my head to listen again, I noticed a pair of black shoes and uniform pants. It was a cop, the first on the scene. "What's up?" he said.

"What's up? I think my wife is having a heart attack. Where are the paramedics?"

The cop told me they were on their way. He stood there and watched as I tried to help my wife. He offered no assistance, no first aid kit, and no oxygen. He came unprepared to a 911 medical emergency. He stood there and watched. He didn't even tell me to step away so he could get involved. Ten minutes later, the paramedics showed up. It was the longest ten minutes of my life.

When the paramedics entered the room, I kissed Dawn and said, "I love you." Shea was crying as the paramedics tried to restore life back into her mother. The paramedics asked me for Dawn's history with medications, ailments, family medical history, and what had happened that night. I gave them the information as they fumbled through their equipment bags. Dawn was gray by then.

The cop who was first on the scene was standing in the doorway as the paramedics worked on Dawn. Was he guarding the scene?

Dawn had suffered from Asthma for years. It was awful. She couldn't breathe on her own. I felt so helpless. I was scared, and the only things that could have helped were a steroid or a breathing treatment.

Dawn was not breathing. Her lips were blue, and the paramedics were asking me for the third time what happened that night. I had told them about dinner, the pecan chicken salad, the ice tea, and the hot bath. "She came in the office, and this happened. Guys! Jesus Christ, she's blue. Give her some fucking oxygen!"

The officer shoved me and said, "Stand back or you're going to jail!"

I was dumbfounded. "Going to jail?" I said. "You wanna have a testosterone contest with me while my wife is dying?"

"Keep it up and you're going to jail," he replied.

I told the officer I wasn't going anywhere and that he should call for backup.

He called for backup.

"How do they let you wear that uniform? You're a disgrace. I teach cops. I have family and friends who are cops. You're no cop."

He said, "Keep it up and you're going to jail."

It was a bad situation. To this day, I don't know why he laid his hands on me. Backup arrived, and it was a totally different energy. The officer was kind, sympathetic, and compassionate.

I went to the back office while the backup officer was speaking to the asshole cop. Dawn was hooked to IVs, and the paramedics were doing chest compressions to restore her heartbeat. I went to check on my daughter. While I was out, the asshole cop went back into the room. I guess he thought he was securing the area.

The paramedics had to tell him to get oxygen!

He lumbered pass me to get it. He took his time. There was no sense of urgency, no hustle, no compassion, and no empathy. He even smirked at me as he passed.

"You piece of shit. That's right. Take your time—it's not your wife dying!"

As he walked on my front lawn to his patrol car, my sister-in-law, my daughter, and I watched him. He opened the trunk and removed the oxygen, which should have been at the scene from the very start.

I was enraged. I followed him and told him what a scumbag he was.

He turned to me and shouted, "You're going to jail." That's the only thing he said to me the entire night. Crazy.

I walked toward him. I was going to hurt him at that point. As a trained martial artist and fighter, I was familiar with grappling, submission holds, chokes, joint locking, weaponry, and weapons disarms. More importantly, I had taught and trained law enforcement. I knew what their training consisted of, and I knew their strengths and weaknesses. I know about the "twenty-one-foot rule."

The twenty-one-foot rule has been a core component in training officers to defend themselves against edged weapons. The rule states that in the time it takes the average officer to recognize a threat, draw a sidearm, and fire two rounds at center mass, an average subject charging at the officer with a knife or other cutting or stabbing weapon can cover a distance of twenty-one feet.

I made a decision that I was going to hurt him. I started my approach to engage him, but as soon I took my first step, my daughter's hand grabbed my shoulder. She said, "No, Daddy. You'll go to jail." My daughter's hand and her voice snapped me back to reality and saved me—and that asshole. I walked away, and that decision stills haunts me to this day. Dawn died shortly after. The cause of death was an aortic aneurysm.

Six weeks later, I made inquiries to friends, family members, and local and state police contacts about that night. They all said the same thing. No one comes to a 911 medical emergency scene unprepared and escalates an already volatile situation. One NYPD detective I have known for more than thirty years said, "Families thank us for helping and rendering assistance during times like that."

I started an internal affairs complaint and told the powers at be that I would not rest and would spend whatever it took to shed light on that travesty. The police department wanted the cop off the force. He had a record of the same thing in the past, and it was an opportunity to terminate him. They investigated, took statements from all those present that night, and found the officer was unprofessional and did not follow proper procedure. He received two weeks of probation. Asshole disputed the findings, and it went to a police trial (by his peers).

My daughter and I would have to relive the events of that night through more investigation, questioning from police administrators, and township prosecutors. At one meeting with a police captain and township attorney, after telling her story of that night, my daughter left two hard-boiled gruff city employees crying.

What if I wasn't a disciplined, focused, stable, honorable man? What if I was a high-strung, nervous, anxious man with little control who drinks to excess and owns a gun? What would have happened that night? My martial arts training protected me and that parasite. My daughter had the focus and intelligence to think for me when I could not. The principles of black belt excellence we both had learned through karate saved us that night. The principles of black belt excellence saved our lives from being torn to bits.

Honesty, courtesy, respect, self-discipline, focus, perseverance, and an indomitable spirit kept my daughter and me grounded and present. These same principles gave us the drive to carry on our lives and be the best we can be.

Our lives were forever changed that night. I was suddenly a single parent with a fifteen-year-old daughter. I also had twelve employees, two businesses, five hundred students, a home, and two dogs.

I have been asked in the past how I did it. I surrounded myself with great people. Jim Rohn said, "You are the average of the five people you spend the most time with."

I made it my mission to be around upbeat, happy, energetic people. I interact with people who are driven and focused. I don't live in the past or the future. I live in the present because that is all that matters. It's been six years since that tragedy, and I still remind myself how there is no handbook when things get crazy. I must be patient and kind with myself. Dr. Stephen Covey said, "Things which matter most should never be at the mercy of things that matter least."

I was thrust into a new world. That new world consisted of making every decision alone—right or wrong, big or small. What dress is appropriate for a junior prom? What bra should my daughter wear with that dress? Who would I put in charge of my affairs if something happened to me? Stephen Covey's advice about which things matter was always on my mind.

We cannot change the cards we are dealt, but we can adjust how we play our hands. I was going to play the hand out and be an example for my daughter. I was going to show her that quitting was not an option. Perseverance and indomitable spirit are not just words to utter; they are words to live by. We honor Dawn by living the best lives we can—full of enthusiasm, passion, honor, kindness, and love.

If I can do it, you can do it. If I can continue to honor Dawn by raising our daughter with morals and values, grow the business as we planned, and spread love, laughter, and kindness to others, you can too. We all have busy lives that are full of distractions and dilemmas. It's a matter of mind-set. We become what we think about. Dr. Wayne Dyer said, "If we change the way we look at things, the things we look at change"

I wanted to set the best example I could for my daughter. I wanted her to see that her father loved her and believed in her. I wanted to instill in her—even during this dark time of losing her mother—that she was endowed with the seeds of greatness. Dawn and I had planted the seeds many years ago. Every night before Shea would fall asleep, I would whisper, "You will be a success. People will see you and say, 'There goes Shea Prendergast. She's somebody important!'"

As parents, we do the best we can. Like you, I'm doing the best I can. Shea is in her third year of college. She is in the honor society and leadership society, and she has made dean's list every semester.

She is thriving. She is kind, confident, and compassionate to others. She wants to help others as a therapist.

Do I need to remind her about cleaning up after herself, car maintenance, laundry, and feeding the dog? Absolutely. That's small stuff. We have a strong foundation, and that's key. I found out that I had to be the change I wanted to see. I came from a childhood filled with criticism, arguments, yelling, and beatings. I decided long ago that I would not pass that down to my child.

Communication, praise, correction, and consistency are the foundation of strong, happy children who grow into happy, productive, respectful adults. I use those words every day to the best of my ability. There is nothing on earth more important than raising my child to be a productive, kind, and thoughtful member of society.

CHAPTER

2

Integrity

Lead your life so you wouldn't be ashamed to
sell the family parrot to the town gossip.
—Will Rogers

I first opened my karate school in Brick, New Jersey, in 1989. It was only 2,500 square feet, and the rent was $2,800 a month. That was all the money in the world to me. My goals were very simple. I wanted to teach enough students so I could pay my rent. If I taught great classes and gave good service, I knew I would eventually be successful and maybe have enough money to go out to dinner once a week. I thought that would be the greatest thing.

Working with children, being in business for myself, making my own hours, being respected, and in a position of authority were the goals I had for myself. I had visions of being popular and respected within the community and having strong ties with the township, especially the police department. I thought establishing rapport with the local police department would give me credibility.

In 1992, there was a tragic and terrible event in the news. A woman from northern New Jersey was carjacked, raped, and murdered. It was news nationwide. Copycat carjackings sent fear into the hearts of men as well as women, and it was all people were talking about. I needed to do something. I decided to do free women's self-defense clinics around the town—to any and all groups who were interested. I decided to enlist the help of the police department. I wanted to educate the public and teach the physical and practical combatives of self-defense. The police would give a lecture, backed up with statistics, about using chemical sprays such as pepper spray and mace.

The police captain was a stern man with no personality. As a former marine, he felt that there were two kinds of people in the world: marines and everybody else. Since I was not wearing a badge or military fatigues, he wasn't very present when I made my pitch for the self-defense classes. Eventually I won him over, and they decided to take a chance on me. We did a seminar for the ladies who worked at town hall and had a great turnout. The successful seminar was a springboard for me. I did many more seminars with the help of my new friends in the police department.

We conducted at least a dozen seminars for hospital workers, parent-teacher organizations, and township employees. The police department was great, and we worked well together. They wanted to reward me with a certificate of merit and a plaque. I was ecstatic. I was looking for testimonials and awards to hang on my walls, and it could not have come at a better time. We set a date, and I thought it would be great if we combined the presentation with a drug-prevention seminar for the kids. I wanted the cops to come in uniform. I thought they could talk to the children and parents about the dangers of drugs. Maybe they could bring the drug-sniffing K-9 officer and give a demo.

My mind was racing with ideas. They all agreed, and the chief of police offered to give me the award. I was excited and so grateful.

When the day came, I was so nervous. I wanted everything to be perfect. The children had to be lined up, sitting properly with chests out, backs straight, and eyes forward. My marine captain cop friend noticed how disciplined they looked.

The children sat at attention and answered each of my questions by saying, "Yes, sir!"

I introduced the captain, the K-9 officer, and other patrolmen.

The police took over, and the K-9 officer began to talk about drugs and the effects of drugs on people. He held up a bag of marijuana and asked, "Does anybody know what this is?"

Kenny was a shy, quiet student who always came to class disheveled and late. He raised his hand and said, "That's weed."

The K-9 officer stared at Kenny and said, "Weed?"

"Yeah, you know, pot. My father grows that in the backyard."

My mouth hit the floor. All the cops, including the chief, stared at me like they had just gotten inside information on a Colombian cartel.

The officer played it off and went on with his presentation. The dog came out, did his thing, and sniffed out the hidden bag of pot.

The chief awarded me the plaque and a certificate for outstanding service to the community. It was a great day, and I was very proud. I didn't think my head could have gotten any bigger when all four officers approached me, thanked me, and praised me for my efforts.

One of them said, "Who's that kid? What's his father's name? Where do they live?"

Oh boy. What should I do? Do I give up the pot-growing father and the six-year-old son to my newfound police department friends— or do I shut my mouth? It was a conundrum. I was new to business, and I needed every student I could get. I was just forming a relationship with the police department, which would give me instant credibility.

I decided to pretend I'd lost my hearing. I stared at them like a deer in the headlights with a blank face and no expression.

The chief said, "Where do these guys live"?

I remembered the line from Goodfellas. When Henry Hill was leaving court, his friends were waiting to congratulate him. Robert DeNiro's character put his arm around Henry and said, "You learned the two greatest things: never rat on your friends and always keep your mouth shut."

I said, "Fellas, please don't put me in this position. Maybe it was parsley or basil the kid saw."

I dodged a bullet. The cops let it go and shook my hand. We went on to do many more events together.

Not long after that, Kenny's father came to the school to pick up his son. I let the father in on what his son had said. He looked at me like he didn't hear me, and then it was his turn to look like a deer in headlights. He didn't say a word to me then—or at any other time after that. Interesting.

When will parents, coaches, leaders, instructors, teachers, and everybody else in positions of influence realize that examples and actions mean more than anything else? At the age of five, Kenny knew nicknames for marijuana and that his father grew it in their backyard.

Jim Rohn was a self-improvement philosopher and business mentor to millions. He said, "You must constantly ask yourself these questions: Who am I around? What are they doing to me? What have they got me reading? What do they have me saying? Where do they have me going? What do they have me thinking? And, most important, what do they have me becoming? Then ask yourself the big question: Is that okay?"

Clinical Wisdom from Carol Davis, LCSW

> Teach your children well, their father's hell did
> slowly go by, and feed them on your dreams, the
> one they picked, the one you'll know by.
> —Graham Nash

It's not every day in my clinical practice, but those days arrive where I want to shout, "Parents, what you are doing to your children?" There is so much knowledge available today about psychology and the development of the brain. Being young happens once, and it is such an important time in a child's life. Children are learning all the time once they leave the comfort of the womb.

Being a parent is one of those roles in life where there is no real manual. It's one of those jobs that seem to never end as children travel through developmental milestones and absorb life's lessons. Herein lies the complexity of this story. Every day, a young child witnessed something illegal in his home. He was not prepared for possible pitfalls, such as his parent getting arrested due to the child's openness.

Children need protection, and I witness this often in my clinical practice when I work with adults who are still mourning the protection they never received as children. What type of protection am I referring too? In today's world, we see overindulgence with children. They have access to information at their fingertips and instant access to their parents. There is virtually no time for young people to develop thinking and coping skills. If they see something, they say it or ask for it. That's why Kenny openly revealed that his father was growing marijuana, which was illegal in New Jersey.

Parents often are unaware of how children absorb information. Exposure to drugs and alcohol at an early age places a child in an at-risk population. Parents need to realize every decision and action they take will have an influence on a child's emotional and social development.

Parents are invested in taking a child to a martial arts class to develop inner strength and master emotions in a productive manner. There is a misperception that emotional strength happens outside of the home with socializing and development of skills like martial arts, sports, dance, and music. I have worked with teachers and coaches who lament the lessons they have to impart on the parents about basic skills. A coach is working on team building, and two parents start fighting or cursing at each other over their children's performance in the game. What are you teaching them? Self-control in an important skill to learn in life, and parents are unable to control the desire for marijuana and shows his child the plants. The child's openness is wonderful, but the child may develop risky behaviors that unknowingly are sanctioned by his parents.

Parents have great power over children's lives. In The Conscious Parent, Dr. Shefali Tsabary reports how parental influence impacts psychology and neurobiology for the remainder of their lives. Dr. Tsabary discusses a common theme in clinical practice. Many people report a metaphorical hunger and thirst for nurturing that only a parent can give. If this thirst is not filled, it does not go away.

Children internalize the voices of their parents, and unconscious parenting hurts children the most. Parents hurt their children because they are hurt and their issues are unresolved. The unresolved issues get passed on to the children. Children trigger unmet needs and challenge their parents on a regular basis. This phenomenon is known as unconscious parenting.

Parents report how painful it is to witness a child in pain. Dr. Tsabary challenges this thinking by asking parents to consider the phenomena of children getting terribly hurt by a parent who cannot be a witness to his or her own pain.

Emotional pain needs to be understood and integrated into your experience in order to evolve as a healthy parent. This is not to suggest in this situation that the parents have hurt this child by growing marijuana. What strikes me is the parent is not aware enough to shield the child from the potential of pain. The adult is not conscious that children need protection and not access to being at risk. Child protection services could have been called, and the police could have intervened. The real danger here is the parent is not even conscious of the effect of his actions.

Parental evolution is the pathway I endorse. I think the greatest gift you can give your child is your own conscious awareness, which means taking care of yourself and being aware of yourself. When children observe their parents dealing with life's trials, they learn a valuable lesson. They learn to accept and honor the experience, which leads to an experience of authenticity. If a parent can accept their own it has inner pain; life could transform for the child. The parent would get help for any unresolved issues and not burden the child with unresolved expectations. In our culture, there is an overemphasis on being happy. We operate with unspoken contracts with our children hoping our children will fulfill the parents' unmet needs (Shefali Tsabary, PhD).

Jeff Foxworthy said, "I know if mama ain't happy, ain't nobody happy." There is tremendous wisdom in this. Parents need to stop focusing on children's scheduled activities and their achievements and focus on themselves. We need to change direction and not focus on success and achievement in our children. We need to understand what we are doing as adults. What we do as adults affects our children.

Book Recommendations

- The Conscious Parent by Shefali Tsabary, PhD
- No Regrets Parenting: Turning Long Days and Short Years into Cherished Moments with Your Kids by Harley Rotbart, MD
- Einstein Never Used Flash Cards by Kathy Hirsh-Pasek, PhD, and Roberta Michnick Golinkoff, PhD

She takes off her shoes.

Referring a friend to your school is the greatest compliment you can pay your instructor and the school. It means you value the teachings of the school, believe in the organization, and want others to benefit as you have.

Twice a year, we have a "Buddy Week" at the school. That week, students can bring a buddy to class. The students bring in friends. The classes are buzzing with energy and good fun. It's electric. I put a spin on Buddy Week and made a contest out of it. Kids love the word contest. When you throw in prizes, forget about it.

Parents love it even more. One mother took it to the extreme. I thought my idea was simple. The student who brought in the most buddies in a week would win a hundred-dollar gift certificate to Toys-R-Us. Absolutely everybody benefits. It's a win-win situation.

The kids get a gold star patch for their uniforms for getting involved, the school gets an infusion of potential new students, and the student who brings the most buddies gets rewarded.

I sent a flyer home with the students to explain the details for Buddy Week. Everyone was excited to bring friends to the school. I even got creative and put together a newsletter for the month. I included it in the monthly itinerary.

Buddy week began on Monday. I bought prizes for the students and buddies and made a chart for the students who brought friends to class. Every time they brought a new friend, they got a sticker on the chart. It was a great incentive, and the kids and parents got to see their progress as well as the progress of others.

The students and parents could check the chart to see the leaders. I had no idea how competitive some mothers could be. John's mother was off the hook. She was bringing in new buddies every day. I thought it was a bit strange because her son was socially challenged. He barely talked and avoided eye contact. He was shy and didn't seem to have many friends, but his mom was bringing multiple friends in every day.

Was she kidnapping random children and bringing them to class? No. She was asking any and all neighborhood kids to come, including his schoolmates, siblings, and cousins. She invited anyone who had kids. She was so into it, and I couldn't have been happier. So many new kids were visiting the school for the first time. I got more leads and potential new students than any advertisement in any paper or magazine could ever bring in.

Bryan was no slouch either. He was in first place, and everyone loved him. He was a standout martial artist and an all-around athlete. In baseball, basketball, football—you name it—he excelled at it. He was polite and liked by his peers. Bringing friends to class was easy. Friday was the last day to bring in buddies. It was a close race between John and Bryan, but Bryan was winning by one.

I reminded Bryan that it was the last day to bring in buddies, but he had no more friends to bring in.

I said, "Congratulations, Bryan. Well done. The contest is over—no more friends please. You did great. Thank you." It was a great week, I couldn't have been happier.

On Saturday, Johnny and his mother checked the board. When they saw that Bryan was still in first place, Johnny's mom sent her two-year-old daughter out to class. The mom ripped off her dirty Velcro sneakers and proceeded into class with the five-year-old students. I think she wore the Velcro sneakers for just that occasion. The mom broke the tie. I almost didn't have the heart to tell her the contest was over and Bryan had won.

Johnny's mother approached me after class and said, "Johnny won. When does he get the hundred dollars?"

I said, "Good morning to you."

"Johnny won, when does he get the hundred dollars?"

"I'm sorry, but Buddy Week ended yesterday. Bryan was the winner. I talked as gently as I could with the biggest smile I could muster.

She produced the newsletter from her purse and wielded it like William Wallace in Braveheart. I felt like a moron. The newsletter said that Saturday was the last day to bring friends. Bryan's flyer said Friday was the last day.

Oops, my fault, my mistake.

She got in my face, looking for a solution to this tragedy in her life. They were affluent people who lived well and wanted for nothing. What could I do to remedy the situation?

I said, "I'm sorry. There was an error in our dates. I will make this right."

My solution, which I thought was reasonable and fair, was to give each boy a fifty-dollar gift certificate, a trophy, and lunch. Bryan and his parents thought that was great. They were very understanding and agreed that it was fair and generous.

Johnny's mother and father believed it was my fault and that I should give each boy a hundred-dollar gift certificate for the mistake.

I agreed it was my error. I also reminded her that Bryan was told to stop, and judging by his past performance, he would have won easily. She took no comfort in that, and Mrs. Dirty Velcro Sneakers was on my last nerve.

I was professional and polite, but she was still arguing in front of the other parents and her own children.

I said, "Madam, may I remind you that this was for the children? You went into a class of five-year-olds to break the tie."

She didn't care. "I know," she said.

We went back and forth for a few minutes. I told her what I was going to do, which was fair—and the other family had no problem with it.

She took the fifty-dollar gift certificate and the trophy. She would not allow her son to take part in the luncheon, but he still attended classes on a regular basis.

She thought I was a poor example of integrity, and she did not want her child to have lunch with the other boy and me. She informed the "troubleshooter" of the Asbury Park Press about my poor business dealings and shady practices.

The mistake was clearly mine, and I owned it. I still can't believe this mother did that with all that was going on in the world and in our daily lives. She felt wronged and showed no flexibility, compromise, or empathy. Her children learned a lesson about conflict resolution.

Life is one big journey with mistakes and obstacles. Things happen. It's best to do what dogs do: no matter what life brings you, kick some grass over that shit and move on.

Clinical Wisdom from Carol Davis, LCSW

In situations like this, it is important to remember that we are not aware of the family dynamic and the potential stress this family may be living with. The mother's motives are unknown except that her child is socially awkward. A child's self-esteem is impacted when parents send a message that is confusing and out of sync with the child's experience.

This child is socially awkward, and his mother is participating in an event for the children to prove her point (competition). Instead of focusing on helping the child develop socially, the mother focused on winning the gift card.

Perhaps money is an issue in this family, which is hidden in this story. There is concern in the culture about the future of children with access to technology and its effects on their lives. This is where the problems are because there is great emphasis on mastery and competition and less focus on the process of living.

When we focus on winning or achieving a goal instead of the learning process, children are at risk in the development of their self-esteem. Everyone cannot win, but the process of participating in a sport or playing on a team is invaluable. These are the experiences that become integrated into the development of a young person. Having an activity like Buddy Week is good for business and wonderful for students.

I cannot stress enough the importance of character development and sharing with a child your delight in witnessing their patience, determination, and bravery. When children develop curiosity about learning and participating in life, they have less anxiety and more self-esteem. There is less focus on reaching a goal and more on enjoying life and learning. The children are beginning to show interest in their own initiatives, which leads them to be curious about life and its offerings.

Again, we are faced with the many challenges of parenting. Being part of a karate class—and an event such as Buddy Week—can enhance a child's self-worth and teach that socialization is as important as competition. Learning to share an experience with a buddy can be a valuable experience for children—even if they are witnessing other children enjoying that experience.

This parent missed an opportunity to model accepting losing with humility, levity, and grace. Losing a game is part of life. Parents need to assist their children in learning this lesson and teach the value of socialization. There is way too much anger and bullying in the world today, and this parent inadvertently taught that lesson.

As stated earlier, we are not privy to the potential stress in the family. Society needs to display more kindness in all situations and teach that kindness matters as much as winning a competition.

You have nothing worth stealing.

Some people believe that if they pay a monthly fee for martial arts lessons, they are entitled to more than martial art lessons. One mom had a child in class and a younger child who would wait in the lobby with her. The young child would scream over anything and everything.

On occasion, I confronted the mother about the screaming. I said, "Is everything okay

When I was really feeling diplomatic, I would say, "Maybe she would like to scream outside. It's a beautiful day."

She said, "Well, with what I pay here, she can scream all she wants."

Therein lies the problem.

From the time Mrs. Sherbert registered her two daughters, she was in a panic. Mrs. Sherbert had been to other karate schools and let me know that her daughters—whom she adopted as babies from Poland—had ADHD. They had been "thrown out" of other schools for poor behavior. At our first meeting, she was a nervous wreck. She was positive I would throw them out too. I explained how we would need to have a private lesson to address their needs. We would use positive reinforcement, our student creed, and our seven home rules for children:

1. Children shall greet their parents with "Hi, Mom! Hi, Dad!" and be sure to say "Good-bye" when they leave.
2. Children will always be respectful to parents, teachers, and elders.

3. Children will be kind to their brothers and sisters.
4. Children will keep the household neat and clean at all times.
5. Children will keep their hair, bodies, and teeth clean daily.
6. Children will not interrupt adult conversations.
7. Children shall fix the recipe for straight As daily.
8. Come home from school, open the refrigerator, and have a glass of milk or juice.
9. Open your book to review what you studied today.
10. Do your homework carefully and properly.
11. Preview what you will study tomorrow.

The lesson went well, and the girls responded to our methods. Mrs. Sherbert signed them up on the spot. She was amazed by how they listened to the other instructors and me. She thought it was a "miracle," and she was "shocked" and "amazed." She even hugged us.

The girls came to class, and like most children with ADHD, they needed to be reminded about the rules. Boundaries needed to be set from time to time, but nothing was out of the ordinary. The only problem that did occur with the children was her inability to correct them effectively without screaming. We could tell when something was wrong as soon as she walked in. She would be red in the face and make a beeline to the front desk. She'd say, "I can't do it," "I don't know anymore," "I've had it," "I'm done," and "I can't." It was exhausting; the problem with the girls was the mother.

When the girls were being silly as young children often do, the mom would have a meltdown. Her lack of patience and anxiety about everything would have her bringing the girls to the front desk to speak to an instructor. As she handed off both girls, she would say, "Here. You take care of it!"

She would speak about her children's shortcomings and poor behaviors to other parents—in front of the girls. It was such weak parenting.

The girls would have good moments as well. The mom would

praise them, but she was more of a dirt digger than a finder of gold. When dealing with people, employees, or anyone you want to influence, you should correct in private and praise in public.

The mom came in crying about every other week. One time, she said, "Jillian is stealing now. My daughter is a thief!" The mom took the girls into a store, and Jillian wanted a toy. The mom said no, and Jillian placed the toy in her pocket. As they walked through the mall, Jillian began playing with her new toy.

The mom began yelling at Jillian, and they left? She said, "I was so embarrassed that I just wanted to get out of there!"

I waited to hear the punishment for shoplifting and defiance. The mom said, "I brought her here to you guys. It's your job to help me."

"Why didn't you make her return the toy?" I asked.

"I didn't want her to get arrested."

All I could think about was what my father and mother would have done in that situation. My father was a strict Irish Catholic, and his father was a New York City cop. My dad had a great respect for law, order, rules, and respect for people and their property. He was the tallest five-foot-six man I've ever known.

My mother was no slouch in that regard either. She was born and raised in England. Her hardworking parents had little education but great values and work ethics. I would have had to return the toy to the manager, and I would have been beaten in the store while returning it. I would have been beaten in the car. When my father got home, I would've have gotten more of the same—not to mention a verbal beating—for the shame I had put on the family name.

I respected and feared my parents because of their methods of parenting. Was their way the right way? I don't know. Maybe. I don't hit my own child, and I have never raised a hand to her. I don't agree with beating a child to make a point or to try to gain their respect through fear and intimidation, but like my parents, I am not my child's buddy or playmate. I am her father. There are consequences for poor behavior and breaking the rules. I praise my daughter when she does well, and I discipline when she does not. I praise, correct, and then praise again.

Jillian and I had a meeting in my office. Jillian's body language said many things to me: indifference, defiance, and lack of remorse. She was so disconnected from what she had done. To say she didn't care was an understatement. She wouldn't talk to me at first, and then she stared right through me.

I asked, "Why would you steal? Do you know that you broke the rules of the school and the student creed?"

She said, "Yeah." When I sit down with young students and confront them with things of this nature, they usually get nervous, cry, and apologize. This girl was cold as ice.

I told her how important and talented she was. I let her know how she had made big improvements, and that I was disappointed. "Jillian, you're a good kid. Do I have to worry about you stealing from me and the others here at the school?"

Jillian looked up at me and said, "There's nothing here worth stealing."

"If there was something worth stealing, would you steal from us?"

"Yes," she said. At ten years old, she was a badass. I couldn't believe what came out of her mouth, and she repeated it for Master Dave. We were gobsmacked by a ten-year-old delinquent.

I had visions of kicking her little ass out of the chair and making her apologize to me—and every student in the school. Instead, I let her know that I didn't want to give up on her. I told her I wanted to help her.

She wanted to quit and not come back.

I said, "Okay. That's fine."

I opened the office door, and the mom was still crying. "You're kicking her out? I knew you would eventually."

"No," I said. "She just kicked herself out. Your daughter told me she doesn't care about what happened, and she said she would steal from me if I had something worth stealing here."

While I was trying to counsel her daughter, she was telling the other parents that I was throwing her out.

The next day, I got a call from Jillian's father. He was a gentle soft-spoken professional who valued the teachings of the school. He believed that the school had helped his daughter immensely, and he did not want her to stop attending. He wanted my help.

I let him know there had to be consequences for her actions. There had to be a price to pay for breaking the rules. She also owed me an apology. He agreed, and we set up an appointment for Jillian to come in with her dad.

Three days later, I met with Jillian and her father. The father was doing all the talking, and he let me know how sorry Jillian was. I could see that she was not sorry. His tone was that of someone who did not wish to upset his daughter. He did not want to hurt his daughter's feelings.

I said, "Your daughter stole, was rude and disrespectful, and broke the student creed and rules of the school." Her punishment would be a loss of rank/demotion, and she would be out of the leadership program (an elite program for students who were leaders inside and outside the school). She also could not use weapons or take specialty classes.

She would then have to earn those privileges back through hard work and a change of attitude. We would restore her rank and privileges when we felt a change had been made.

"I'm not doing that!" Jillian said.

"Can we go home and think about it?" the dad asked.

Think about it? Are you out of your frigging mind? "Sure," I said. "Think about it as long as you like, but if you want to remain at the school, this is what it is."

The dad thanked me and said he would be in touch.

The following day, he called me. The family had discussed the punishment and felt it was too harsh. They asked me to reconsider.

I said, "No. I'm sorry, but that would send a bad message to her and everyone else. And seeing that your wife told the parents in the lobby what she had done, I cannot overlook this. What would you have me do?"

He said, "Maybe she could go to the next two classes without her belt—and don't say it's a punishment because we don't want to embarrass her."

I laughed and said, "Can't do that." I stuck to my guns, got the cold shoulder from the mom for the next week. She brought the other daughter to two classes and harassed the instructor about when Jillian could get her belt back.

She thought we were being too harsh by embarrassing her daughter and damaging her psyche. We were the villains? By week two, the mom had had enough of my cruel and embarrassing punishment. She asked when Jillian could regain her belt and privileges.

The instructor said, "Once Master Paul feels an improvement has been made."

The mom pulled her daughters out of class and stormed out of the school.

The dad came into the school the following day to cancel their program. To his credit, he was a gentleman. He thanked me for all we had done. With a tear in his eye, he left like a broken and defeated man.

The other daughter had been making huge improvements and getting better in every way. Jillian was collateral damage from her mother's poor decision. Our decisions in life help shape our destinies. It would not surprise me if I heard about Jillian getting in trouble with the law or doing damage to herself or others. I hope the mom will awaken from her delusional slumber and become proactive. A present, patient, and loving parent believes that accountability and respect are paramount—and that discipline teaches lessons.

Clinical Wisdom from Carol Davis, LCSW

> The possessions themselves were not the problem—
> it was my relationship with possessing.
> —Chris Matakas, author of #Human:
> Learning To Live in Modern Times

What does bad behavior mean? As a therapist, I always wonder what children or young adults are expressing when they exhibit behavior that inevitably brings attention and consequences. The children think the adults missed them again. They can continue to hide out and not really be seen or heard.

In this scenario, the child is not referring to possessions. The child was adopted from Poland into a loving home, but the parents were not prepared for the process and perhaps had not let go of the notion that life was going to have some tumult. I always counsel parents in this situation to put on their seat belts. I inquire about their expectations of the adoption.

In situations where parents cannot have biological children, it is common not to have grieved. We are not aware of the circumstances, but the child in this situation is waiting for the relationship to emerge. The child is waiting for the parents to meet her where she is. Problems emerge because the child is not exactly where they would like her to be. In the story, the children are always getting thrown out.

Jillian is searching for a connection and for someone to understand that her behavior is not the problem (despite the interruptions and reactions she encounters). The problem is the relationship because there is no relating go on. She will continue to pose questions until someone understands her loss. Reckless behavior and aggression will be her friends because she cannot visualize a connection. The adults need to be connectors and help Jillian navigate her life, which was lost through her early life experience.

In My Mastery: Learning to Live through Jiu Jitsu, Chris Matakas discusses a concept that he refers to as "killing the monster when it's small." In ancient times, if you came across a dragon egg in a village, you would be better off killing the egg before it becomes a fiery dragon. Parents are faced with this challenge every day with their children. They must teach and mold their children's lives. This child came from a foreign country with emotional baggage and social history. Parents need to understand where their children came from in order to help them not emerge as dragons. The principle is helpful for parents because it is useful. Life is full of monsters.

Adopted children experience change and transition during adoption. Some children from foster care, disorganized orphanages, institutions, and refugee camps experience abuse and neglect and have tremendous difficulty trusting and bonding with caregivers. These disorders are known as reactive attachment disorder (RAD) or disinhibited social engagement disorder (DSED). According to the DSM-5 (the American Psychiatric Association's classification and diagnostic tool), the frequency of RAD in high-risk populations is less than 10 percent; DSED is about 20 percent. Both disorders present with multiple behavior issues consisting of emotional withdrawal, inhibition, impulsiveness, social disturbance, mood swings, and a prevailing distrust of caregivers, which could include parents, teachers, and coaches. These disorders are generally diagnosed in children under the age of five. In my experience, the key factor in treating these children and families is working with the families and helping strengthen the relationship with empathy and building communication. Each child and parent is different. Treatment needs to be tailored to the needs presented. I encourage parents to put on their seat belts.

If I were working with this family, my primary focus would be the parents. Jillian's mom has not accepted her child and is reacting to her behavior in a confusing manner. Jillian continues to get attention (positive and negative), and she feels reassured that she is not alone. However, she is absorbing antisocial tendencies, and Jillian's dad seemingly has limited parental power. The parents need to come together and work as a team to give Jillian a chance to succeed. I would also provide emotional support and empathy to the parents since it is extremely difficult to raise a child who often rejects your love because of early childhood experiences. If adoptive parents have not resolved their own losses over not having biological children, this is crucial for success with adopted children. It is possible to succeed, but there is work to be done in therapy.

Diagnostic and Statistical Manual of Mental Disorders, Fifth Edition, American Psychiatric Association, (2013).

Not in my backyard.

In 1994, a little girl from Hamilton, New Jersey, was raped and murdered by her neighbor. Megan Kanka was lured to a neighbor's house a mere thirty yards from her doorstep under the ruse of seeing a puppy. Unknown to the Kanka family, a convicted sex offender lived across the street. The murderer had already served six years in prison for aggravated assault and attempted sexual assault on another child.

Months after this heinous crime was committed, a nationwide law was passed. The law required notification when a convicted sex offender moved into a neighborhood. The law protects families and their children.

Megan could have been anyone's child. This terrible tragedy sent fear into the hearts of every parent I knew. Parents at my karate school were even more protective. Stricter precautions were put in place in every business and school that dealt with children and families. It forced everyone to reevaluate who they trusted their children with. It forced everyone to take a good, hard look at what their children were doing, where they were going, who they had friendships with, and who they associated with.

Some parents were over the top. They wanted fingerprinting of instructors they had trusted and liked for years. They wanted video cameras in classrooms for surveillance, and some even wanted background checks. It was a fearful and crazy time. Normal, levelheaded, reasonable people were scared and doubtful.

As a parent, I totally understood the concerns of the families that attended my school. We all moved forward though. What could we do other than be a bit more cautious and more present with our children? Not a bad thing.

It was a busy day at the school. On Fridays, the students were sparring. Kids were coming and going and trying to put on their sparring equipment. Instructors and parents were helping the children with their equipment. For the five-year olds, it was a big deal.

In the middle of all this organized chaos, there was always a parent who had forgotten something or needed something. A woman told me that her brother would be picking up her two boys after class. He was a registered sex offender who had just completed his prison sentence.

"Excuse me?" I said. "Could you repeat that please?"

"I just wanted to let you know that my brother is on Megan's List. He's served his sentence. He's okay now—and he's gonna pick up the boys after class, okay?"

Is she for real? You can't make this shit up. Her brother was coming into the school—a busy school that would be filled with young children. That's kinda like letting the wolf into the henhouse. I stared at her and said, "No, he's not. Sorry. He's not welcome here."

She was dumbfounded and wanted to know why. She thought I was being harsh and unsympathetic to her plight. Her brother had served his debt to society, and I wasn't embracing him as a redeemed man. I was okay with that.

"Sorry. Out of respect to the many families that attend—and in light of what has happened recently—I cannot and will not permit your brother to enter this school. I do not want to see him around it or the students."

You can't fix stupid.

She worked it out and was able to pick up her children.

What about her own children? She had two boys, and she was

entrusting her children to this man. She was a better person than I was. I don't think I would ever do that or be comfortable with it.

Clinical Wisdom from Carol Davis, LCSW

Childhood sexual abuse is an area in my practice that I have grown to understand since I have worked with numerous survivors. In some respects, it has been an honor to witness folks healing such deep wounds from childhood.

I urge people to educate themselves about the intricate issues involved with these families. There is a phenomenon within family systems of sexual abuse of profound denial and no safety provided for children.

Denial is a powerful and primitive defense mechanism that exists in situations of sexual abuse. How does that happen? Most survivors have a range of emotions toward the perpetrators: love, anguish, hatred, rage, confusion, fear, loyalty, and longing (Laura Davis, 1991). This is not to suggest that survivors like the abuse. It is complicated due to the attachment to family and a fear of losing family, which is common theme. By disassociating from the abuse, a survivor is able to maintain a semblance of family. I have treated many survivors, and my experience has shown me that sexual abuse can be a terrifying betrayal. The survivors often prefer living as if it did not happen. The mom informed Master Paul—with limited emotion—about the pickup arrangements for her two children, which included alarming information about her brother. This psychological phenomenon is known as psychic numbing. The mom is able to disassociate from her feelings in order to preserve a relationship with her brother.

Child sexual abuse is a violent physical attack. Victims often suffer long-term effects, resulting in trauma-filled lives. It is similar to other forms of violence since the victim is subjected to an act of aggression that utilizes power and aggression. It is a classic example of the powerful overcoming the weak. Parents have become more educated, and Megan's law is an outcome of advocacy and education.

There remains much education for parents to be aware of regarding sexual abuse. Again, I urge parents to communicate with your children and listen to their language and their behavior. Children will often express their experience in some form, and it is our job as parents to receive that communication. I recognize that it is easier said than done.

Another reason there is widespread denial about childhood abuse is that society and the public do not want to accept the crime of sexual abuse as being so prevalent. It is our responsibility as neighbors, families, friends, teachers, coaches, and school officials to report suspected abuse to the authorities. A rule of many abusive families is silence, and families adhere to this rule. It cannot hurt to be wrong, and it could help a child if there is abuse going on. In this situation, Master Paul advocated for the children by informing the mom that her brother was not allowed at the school. It illustrates the magnitude of abuse within families and how denial exists even with the knowledge that her brother was a convicted sex offender.

There is hope for healing for survivors of sexual assaults—even though the journey to healing may be rocky. It is important to work with families and survivors with compassion and a nonjudgmental stance. There are many factors to understand about this issue. Unfortunately, sexual abuse does exist in our backyards. I encourage parents to learn more about it since it is so prevalent.

Society is more educated about psychological trauma than it was in the past. In order to understand the complexity of sexual abuse, I turn your attention to traumatic bonding, another phenomena that exists within sexual abuse. Traumatic bonding occurs within family systems when family members deny and minimize an abuser's behavior by normalizing the relationship. It's important to understand because it leaves children in dangerous predicaments. There is a bond, and only someone outside of the system can see the danger.

With prisoners of war, traumatic bonding exists within captivity. In our culture, it is more difficult to understand sexual abuse and domestic violence within family systems. I urge you to invoke more understanding if you encounter survivors. If hostages with no prior connection to their captors can bond traumatically, imagine how complex it is for a child with a parent or caregiver. There are many factors involved, but there are many books about sexual abuse.

As a society, advocacy for potential victims can even present itself in a karate school, which is what occurred.

Suggested Readings

Allies in Healing: When the Person You Love Was Sexually Abused as a Child by Laura Davis

Trauma and Recovery: From Domestic Abuse to Political Terror by Judith Herman

A Candy Cane and a Black Belt

People quit things. It's inevitable. They quit diets, gyms, marriages, jobs, and karate. It happens. When a student quits taking my karate class, I take it personally. It's like I've been fired. I fell short in some area and failed them.

Teaching is a personal thing. It's sharing yourself, your knowledge, and your expertise. When a student quits, you can't help but look within yourself to how you could have done better. But when students quit because they did not receive a candy cane or didn't get to wear the instructor's black belt for doing a good job in class, I don't feel like I failed the student. I feel like the parents have failed their children.

This story takes place around Christmas. We were teaching a children's class of five- and six-year-old children. The class was full, the instructors were energetic and on point, and the class was having a good time. The children were present and engaging. The instructor decided to end the class on a high note by having the children do relay races. The winning team would receive candy canes as a prize.

Team A was fast and energetic. They worked well together and won. Team B did well and had great effort, but they lost. In competition, someone wins—and someone loses. Team A received candy canes, and the children on the losing team acted accordingly.

Larry made faces and stormed off the dojo floor. He was five, and I got it. I didn't get why Larry's mother called me the next day to say they were quitting. Larry was doing well. Larry's mother enrolled him for discipline and focus. That was her objective. When I asked why they were quitting, Larry's mother said, "He didn't get a candy cane, and he won't go back to class." She told me how unfair it was that the other kids received candy canes, and it wasn't right to upset him.

"Oh my," I replied. I was in shock since she wanted our help with her son's discipline and behavior.

I tried to reason with mom, and I reminded her that everyone can't always win. There is a lesson to learn when one loses. She didn't want to hear it. She hung up the phone. I lost a student over a candy cane.

Henry David Thoreau said, "If one advances confidently in the direction of their dreams, and endeavors to live the life he has imagined, he will meet with a success unexpected in common hours."

I love this quote. If more parents advanced confidently in the direction of their dreams of being the parents they imagined themselves to be, we would have fewer problems with our children. Many of these problems could have been corrected.

About 90 percent of the parents who walk into my schools want their children to learn focus, discipline, confidence, and self-respect. And then they forget.

James was a spirited six-year-old boy. His mother was recently divorced and was doing the best she could with two children and a job as a teacher. She wanted improvement in James's behavior. He had trouble listening and keeping his hands to himself. James wanted what he wanted, when he wanted it, and he wanted it now! That was why his mother enrolled him.

Classes at my school are informative and upbeat, and they have fun drills. Instructors sometimes offer their own belts as a reward for hard work and effort. Wearing an instructor's belt can be empowering for them. It lifts their spirits and pumps them up.

James wanted the instructor's belt. Unfortunately, the belt went to another student who had hustled and shown greater effort that day. James and his mother left after his class like any other day. They gave me no indication that there was a problem until the next day. The mother called to let me know that James was quitting.

"James is upset that he didn't get the instructor's belt in class yesterday. He doesn't want to go back to class."

The little darling who was at the school for discipline and behavior was calling the shots?

Instant gratification hurts so many of us. Some adults are still affected by it. I must have the boat, the car, the watch, and I must have it now—even if it means I go further and further into debt. Letting James quit was a big mistake. He wanted what he wanted; when he didn't get it, he quit. She didn't want to hear my thoughts about how letting him quit was just fueling what we were trying to correct. She was firm and decisive with me, but she couldn't be firm and decisive with her own son. The son was running the house and calling the shots. James won, and the mom lost.

Clinical Wisdom from Carol Davis, LCSW

Difficult people are often unaware that they are being difficult. They view the world solely from their perspectives. Their behaviors may stem from personal histories, worldviews, and habitual patterns. It is possible that the mom was triggered into self-protective defenses by reminders of past difficulties or traumas. It is absurd that it came from a moment in her five-year-old's life when he was disappointed that he did not get a candy cane. She may never have been challenged to examine her difficult behavior due to her social, economic, or professional status. It is possible that she was locked into habituated patterns that indicate a strong need to control and overpower others.

In this situation, we are faced with attempting to understand behavior and communication styles. Aggressive and passive characteristics are frequently found in difficult people who are raising children. Most people will experience frustration and aggression during some point in their lives. This child was disappointed in the activity at the karate school, which could potentially be a good learning lesson for a child. Teaching children compassion, ambition, empathy, fairness, and the limits of their abilities can be valuable.

Growing up, I was always on the swim team. Even though I was not a champion swimmer, I gained so much from being part of a team and facing failure. Swimming became part of the fabric of my life, and I thrived when I had access to a pool. This young boy missed the life lesson on many levels. Being upset and facing disappointments can prepare a child for life's trials and joys. This experience could have been a gift for this child that would last a lifetime. The goal of karate school was to achieve focus and discipline; sadly, these goals were not met.

Parents need to realize that controlling situations for your children to always have a positive outcome sets them up to become aggressive people. The challenge for parents is taking the time to talk to your children and help them accept life's frustrations and achievements. I have listened to many parents who admit that indulging their children was easier than taking the time and energy to assist them in growing up.

Hymel, KP, (1996) *Pediatrics in Review,* Child Advocacy Team, University of Colorado Health Sciences Center, Denver, Colorado

Klykylo, M. and Kay Jerald, (2012) *Clinical Child Psychiatry, Third Edition,* Chapter 18, Elimination Disorders: Enuresis and Encopresis John Wiley & Sons, London, 2012,

3

Honesty

No legacy is so rich as honesty.
—William Shakespeare

Poo Picasso

I've never really been artistically blessed. I was a classical trained chef prior to owning a martial arts school. Being artistically blessed might have served me well when I had pastry class or when I did ice carvings.

I've always been quite envious of those fortunate souls who can create pictures or drawings, play musical instruments with ease, or use their talents in the trades.

I was not a fan of "Poo Picasso," but I'm sure he thought he was quite talented.

As a martial arts instructor, there are days when you are called upon to do unpleasant jobs. This day was one of those. Some students say, "My belly hurts," or "I have a headache," or "can I go to the bathroom?" I let them sit for a moment or go to the bathroom. After a brief time-out, we get back to work, have some fun, and learn something.

William was a quiet, eight-year-old boy who always seemed to have a lot on his mind. During class, William raised his hand and asked to be excused. He bowed out to the instructor and went to the bathroom.

I noticed that William was gone for quite some time. I handed over the class to my assistant and went to check on William. I gently knocked on the door so I didn't startle him, and I used my gentle voice to say, "William, are you okay in there?"

"Yes," he said.

"You've been in there a long time. Do you need help?"

"I'm good."

He hesitated before he answered me, and I asked, "Can I come in?"

"Sure," he said.

I opened the door, and William was covered in poo. It was on him, on the floor, on the walls, and even on the mirrors! How'd he get it on the mirrors? I was dazed and confused, but I knew stomach bugs could be a nasty business. William must have had a stomach bug.

"Not feeling well, buddy?"

He said, "I'm fine, sir." He didn't falter.

I said, "William, don't move." I didn't want it traveling anywhere else at this point. I grabbed him a new uniform from the supply closet and told him to clean himself up in the other bathroom as I surveyed the damage.

With my hand over my mouth and nose, I surveyed his artwork. He had smeared it on all of the walls. He made great lines and images, good arcing, linear lines with brilliant movement. He even got creative and used the mirror to make more of an abstract look.

I had William put the soiled uniform in a trash bag and gave him some cloths and soap. With a bucket of water, I helped William get clean and somewhat hygienic and presentable for his parents.

I ducked out to call his parents and inform them about what had happened. "Hi, this is Master Paul. I think William is under the weather and needs to be picked up."

His mom asked me what the problem was.

"I think he has a stomach bug. He had an accident and soiled himself."

"Not my son!"

"Yes. I'm sorry. It was William."

"Not my son. He wouldn't do that!"

I didn't say about his artwork, my mirrors, or changing clothes.

I finally said, "I know who you are, and I know your son. He's had an accident all over the bathroom. Come get him and take him home."

The lingering fumes must have made me stern in my speech. I had to describe her son to her because she didn't believe me.

After we hung up, I was even more lightheaded. How could his mother be that way? I went back to check on Poo Picasso, and he looked all shiny and new in a clean uniform.

His father arrived and said, "Okay, William, let's go home."

No thanks? No apology?

I put down my mop, took off my rubber gloves, and handed him the bag with William's soiled clothes.

"Thanks," he said, and off they went.

I was not looking for tears and a thousand accolades about how wonderful I was for cleaning up after his child, but I hoped he would acknowledge the kindness I showed to his child. What goes on in that family's house? Why would he take his own poo, draw on the walls of his karate school, and be calm about it? Why wasn't he embarrassed? Why weren't his parents embarrassed? Why weren't his parents shocked or sympathetic to their child?

It is my sincerest hope and prayer that this was not the case for my student. He continued to go to class, and his parents never mentioned what had happened. I want to encourage parents to seek help with mental health professionals, which is why I have included clinical wisdom throughout the book. Reflecting on this situation, I realize he needed help and was expressing it through his behavior.

Clinical Wisdom from Carol Davis, LCSW

> Denial ain't just a river in Egypt.
> —Mark Twain

The defense mechanism called denial is often used when people are unable to face reality or an obvious truth. Denial is a way to refuse what is happening because it is too painful or there is helplessness present. This young boy is expressing himself via smearing feces; unfortunately, his parents are not responding to his communication. It is not clear from this story if this is symptomatic of a psychological problem or if it stems from autistic behavior. However, it is clear that his family is not recognizing the severity of Master Paul's experience in the bathroom.

Encopresis is basically a repeated passage of feces into inappropriate places, such as on the floor or in clothing. Typically, the passage is involuntary in nature, but it can be intentional in some situations (Klyko & Kay 2012). Encopresis is not a disease; it is a symptom that may have different causes. The diagnostic criteria can be found in the DSM-5.

Involuntary passage of feces after the age of four requires physical evaluation to rule out constipation issues and other physical problems. There are family situations that are associated with encopresis, and I cannot overemphasize that every situation is different. The following list includes examples of situations that could suggest the possibility of encopresis (Cohen 2011):

- abuse or neglect
- diet that is rich in fat and/or sugar
- inadequate water intake
- presence of chaos or unpredictability in the patient's life
- lack of physical exercise
- refusal to use the bathroom, especially public restrooms
- presence of a neurological impairment

- history of constipation or painful defecation
- cognitive delays, such as, autism or mental retardation
- presence of obsessive/compulsive disorders
- ADHD or difficulty focusing
- learning disabilities

As you can see, the psychological issue is not clearly defined. However, it is clear that the child is expressing a problem. Often, parents are ashamed of this behavior, and it is typical to deny the behavior initially. In reviewing the literature on psychological interventions, it is highly recommended that family therapy be considered since children presenting encopresis typically are suffering with other stressors, including conduct problems, emotional problems, eating disorders, and somatic problems. Some parents need supportive interventions and education (Carr, 2014).

If I were a therapist in Master Paul's school, I would suggest a meeting with both parents. It is estimated that by the age of eighteen, 12 to 25 percent of girls and 8 to 10 percent of boys have been victims of sexual abuse (Hymel KP, Child JG. Child sexual abuse. Pediatric 1996 17: 236–250). There is reason for concern when children exhibit behavioral changes or have anogenital or medical problems.

Encopresis and enuresis are common medical problems in abused children. It is essential that a professional conduct an interview because of the nature of the issue, and the problem could stem solely from medical reasons. Of utmost importance is maintaining an atmosphere devoid of shame and punishment, encouraging the child and parents that there is hope. Often the child in abuse situations is expressing the lack of control in their lives.

I would recommend continuing martial arts and provide some solutions for the parents. An assessment can help the child express himself. I would explain to the parents that this is a crisis, and I see crisis as an opportunity to understand and help the child achieve mastery in his life. This is not a phase; it is an expression of unexpressed emotion, which can be from psychological stressors or neurological stressors.

It is very treatable. Intervening in children's lives when they demonstrate problems is extremely helpful. In the long run, they remember that their communications were received and help was provided.

I suggest the following guidelines:

☐ Realize this behavior is time limited and needs a gentle, confident approach. It's best to not discuss details with the child and magnify the horrific nature of the feces or bed-wetting.

☐ Let the child draw pictures regarding this behavior and introduce the concept of choices the child could make when stressed. Books and arts and crafts projects can be useful for parents and children.

☐ Satisfy the child's curiosity and interest in poop in a more appropriate way. Books such as Everyone Poops by Taro Gomi can be helpful.

Kids Health.org, Soiling Encopresis
Children's Sexual Behaviours: A Parents Guide The Sources
Provincial Child Sexual Abuse Advisory Committee 2013
Contemporary Psychotherapy "Martial Arts And Mental Health"
Julius-Cezar Macaine and Ron Roberts
"My Kid is smearing feces!" by Tara Mc Clintick 2015
Diagnostic Criteria DSM-5 2013 American Psychiatric Association

The Abused Child

A child who has been sexually abused or has had significant physical abuse such as horrendous beatings on their buttocks can be emotionally cut off from any bodily sensations below their waist.

By cutting off from the awful pain, the child loses the ability to recognize body signals to defecate.

There is also another argument that the child almost uses faecal smearing as a defense against being sexually abused, as this is a powerful way of keeping the perpetrator away from them.

Faecal smearing can indicate early traumatic experiences that a child cannot put into words. It can be their only way of showing their distress.

For a person caring for a child who is smearing e.g. foster parent, it`s important that they let the child know that they understand how upset the child is, and are trying to work with the child to help them look at different ways they can communicate their upset. Its best to avoid asking the child to say why they smear—if they could put those feelings into words then they would not need to resort to smearing. It`s also important to remember that smearing is not a deliberate act of defiance. To the child smearing can make sense of what happened to them in the past and the behavior is very much a way for them to express their unhappiness in what has happened to them in the past, not as a reaction to them for where they are now."

—"Faecal Smearing," netmums.com

Carr, Alan (2014) "The Evidence-Base for Family Therapy and Systemic Interventions for Child-Focused Problems," *Journal of Family Therapy.*

Cohen, Esther (2011) *The Treatment of Encopresis in Children, Integrating a Behavioral Approach with Medical, Strategic, and Relational Considerations.* Probook Publishers, Israel.

Diagnostic and Statistical Manual of Mental Disorders, Fifth Edition (2013), American Psychiatric Association.

Looking for a Payday?

Traditionally, the Japanese arts focuses on three main components: Kihons, Kumite, and Kata. Kihons are the essential self-defense techniques that correspond with an attacker's grabs and attacks. Kumite is the sparring or fighting aspect. Kata is the dance-like performance where the Kara-te-ka (practitioner) uses kicks, blocks, and punches in an arranged movement. This class was practicing the "Kumite" component (sparring). Students either love sparring—or they hate sparring. The students who don't like confrontation or physical contact usually have problems with sparring, but it is essential for developing a well-rounded student in the martial arts.

When students spar, they wear protective equipment—and it is a lot more than I ever had. They wear headgear, shin pads, foot pads, mouthpieces, hand pads, groin protectors, and chest guards. When I was coming up the ranks, we had gloves. Our gloves were more like socks pulled over our hands with a piece of foam rubber underneath. We also had a groin cup, and that was about it. My insurance carrier determines the equipment my students use.

This sparring class was an adult class—fifteen and up—and chest protectors were not a mandatory piece of equipment. When conducting a sparring class, you need to have eyes everywhere—and you have to control the floor. You must do as the instructor says and pair students together accordingly, especially if they're just learning to spar. I love to spar. I love what I do, and there are days when teaching a group of seasoned and experienced students allows me the opportunity to work with the upper ranks.

Gary was four weeks away from testing for his black belt. Gary had more than four years of experience with me, and he had spent another eighteen months at a competitor's school prior to coming to me.

Gary's dad was concerned that Gary wasn't being challenged enough and asked if I would work with him on his sparring. The dad thought Gary needed to be "toughened up some more."

I said, "Sure. I'd be happy to work with him."

Gary's dad was a Monday-morning quarterbacks who could tell you everything about the sport—and how it should be done better—even though he never played a sport. Since he worked in the maintenance department for the local football team, he thought he was an authority. I accommodated him, put on my gloves, jumped into the class, and sparred with my students.

Line sparring is a common drill. Students pair up and spar at 50 percent speed and power. After two minutes, the round is over. The students rotate to the student to the right, and it repeats until everyone gets to spar with everyone. This great drill is used in most schools.

In 1994, there was this new sport on pay-per-view. In Ultimate Fighting Championship, fighters from different martial arts test their skills in an octagon cage. Boxers, sumo wrestlers, kick-boxers, Brazilian jujitsu practitioners, and karate fighters beat the hell out of each other—with no equipment and only bare knuckles. A Brazilian jujitsu player would shoot in on his opponent (dive at the legs), tie him up, and choke him out. It was effective against fighters who had no knowledge of grappling.

Gary was a huge fan of this new sport. When it was my turn to spar with him, tried to shoot in for a takedown. Gary had no experience with single-leg takedowns or any wrestling techniques. He shot in on me, and I sprawled to void his attack. I instantly stopped the match and ask, "What are you doing?"

"I'm trying a takedown."

I explained how that sacrifice move was very dangerous for a novice—and not really recommended for someone so small, especially against a much larger opponent. Gary was 125 pounds soaking wet and five foot five inches tall.

"With someone my size, stick to the basics. If you shoot in, you could eat a kick to the face," I said.

He attempted the takedown a second time. I was shaking my head and watching the rest of the class. I weigh 260 pounds, and I'm six foot two. Some people consider that a big guy, and I hold the rank of sixth dan, master instructor. I'm a former wrestler and a jujitsu practitioner. Why wasn't he listening to me? He had moxie. I said, "What are you doing? Nice thought. Don't shoot in!"

We sparred for a few more seconds, and he attempted the same moronic takedown that he had seen on pay-per-view. I kneed him in the chest, and Gary went down. Gary was having trouble catching his breath.

I brought Gary back to my office, let him rest on the couch, and applied some ice to the area.

His dad came back and said, "Jesus Christ, Gary. You walked right into that!"

Gary was still in pain and was having trouble breathing. I recommend a trip to the ER for X-rays. His father was unfazed and told me he would let me know what the doctor said.

I called the next day to check on Gary, but there was no answer. I called again the next day. On my third try, his mom said Gary was fine. The doctors had kept him overnight for observation. They were being cautious.

Earlier that month, a boy playing baseball was hit in the chest with a pitch, suffered a heart attack, and died. It made sense that the doctors were acting cautiously. I thought I'd send a get-well card and a small gift.

The following week, Gary and his father sued me for $750,000. The complaint was filed in Superior Court. When I started to read the complaint, I became sick. The complaint used words like "inflicted pain and suffering," "intentional harm," "traumatized," "can't live life as he knows it," and "willfully and purposely."

I was shocked and saddened. In all my years of training and teaching, I had never been in a situation like that. No one had ever accused me of intentionally inflicting pain and suffering. Sparring has contact. It's like wanting to play football and getting upset when you're tackled. It didn't make any sense to me. The father had asked me to work with him and to challenge him. I told the boy on several occasions not to shoot in for a takedown. He had four years of experience with me. He also had some boxing experience. Why the sudden turnaround?

The timing could not have been worse. Dawn and I were having our first child, and it was a complicated pregnancy from the start. During the emotionally draining, time-consuming lawsuit, the opposing lawyer referred to me as "husky." During the deposition, they tried to get me to admit and/or discover evidence that they could use to their advantage prior to court. They kept bringing up a time when I had to speak to Gary and another student about their conduct and disrespect to a classmate.

It was no big deal. They were rude and disrespectful to another classmate. I overheard what they said and asked them to come to my office. I said, "We don't speak to each other like that. You guys are upper ranks—act like it." Was I stern and to the point? Absolutely. Did I want them to know they were wrong and language like that would not be tolerated? Absolutely.

They used that incident—the only time I ever had any negative moment with Gary—as a reason to sue me. This incident occurred a month before Gary got hurt. They thought I had some ax to grind with them. They thought I purposely hurt him because of our prior discussion. What bullshit. Like I said to his lawyer when cross-examining me, "If I wanted to hurt him, I could have—very easily." Such nonsense. Dawn and the baby were in questionable health. There were frequent and multiple visits to the high-risk baby doctors.

How hurt was Gary? He had no broken bones, no nerve damage, no internal injuries, no torn ligaments, and no torn muscles. He had a possible fractured sternum. They had no conclusive reports. The x-rays were negative. The MRIs were negative. The doctors had nothing. It was a bruised chest. That was it. A bruise. I asked my attorney why they were doing it if they had no injuries to speak of.

"They're looking for a payday. How long have you been in business?"

"Almost seven years," I replied.

My attorney knew of people who were in business for much less time who have been sued multiple times. It didn't make me feel any better, but I guess that was what happened in business.

During the deposition, their attorney produced a picture of a chest protector. In his most pompous and arrogant voice, he said, "Ever seen this, Mr. Prendergast?"

"Yes," I said.

"Have you ever offered these to your students?"

"No," I replied.

That knucklehead went on about chest protectors and how I should offer chest protectors if I truly cared about my students' health and welfare.

My answer was simple. I had never worn one, and I believe it gives a false sense of security to participants. I compared it to how NFL football players have so much equipment and propel themselves at each other like projectile missiles. They have a false sense of security because of the helmets. The injuries are ridiculous, and they're outfitted from head to toe.

We went to arbitration, and a panel of lawyers decided if the case should go to trial. They agreed that the case shouldn't go to court. Their attorney was beside himself. He tried to cut a deal in the hallway—classic bottom-feeder and stereotypical ambulance chaser. It went from $750,000 to $300,000, and then it dropped to $125,000.

I was not settling. I wanted my day in court. I was pissed. They asked for help and then sued me.

The case never went to court. My record spoke for itself, and another lawyer on the panel advised the opposing attorney not to go forward with it because of my impeccable reputation and unblemished business record. That was nice to hear.

Gary did get $3,000 because I didn't tell him to wear a chest protector. It was my fault because I didn't tell him about chest protectors and how he should buy one.

Gary signed up for lessons at a Brazilian jujitsu studio a week after he got hurt. After he was "traumatized, intentionally and maliciously hurt, and can't live life as he knows it," he enrolled at another school. So much for being traumatized. What was even worse was the lesson that weasel of a man was teaching his son. Let's not be accountable for our actions and blame others. Let's try for a payday. Let's work the system. Let's lie and fabricate. I wonder if Gary will pass this down to his sons or daughters one day? Instead of being a beacon of honesty, integrity, and good will, Gary's father has shown his son a path of deceit, ill will, and pettiness.

Clinical Wisdom from Carol Davis, LCSW

> Your children are not your children. They are the sons and
> daughters of life's longing for itself. They come through you but
> not from you. And though they are with you, yet they belong
> not to you. You may house their bodies but not their souls.
> —Kahlil Gibran, The Prophet

Having a child is a life-changing and miraculous gift. There are often not words to describe the joy and the realization that life is bigger than one ever imagined. Raising a child requires honesty, dedication, tireless emotions, and desire for your child to achieve and surpass your achievements. Zealousness can overcome parents, and it is important to be aware of who your child is. Their gifts and talents may be different from yours. In my experience working with children and families, I encourage parents to consider their expectations of their children.

As Kahlil Gibran writes, "We do not own our children." There is a responsibility to teach them respect for themselves, respect for others, and personal safety. In this situation, it appears that Gary is fulfilling his father's expectations of him to fight Master Paul and "take him down" even though it is totally unrealistic and unsafe to attempt. In my opinion, the child is being used to demonstrate a point. Child-rearing attitudes include cognitions that can lead parents to behave positively or negatively toward children. These predictors of parenting behavior determine the emotional climate in which parents and children operate and how good the relationship is. In this situation, I would venture a guess that the parent is driving the child to perform in order to prove something that was unfulfilled in his own life. We need to be mindful of our attitudes and unresolved issues when raising children.

In The Unconscious Parent, it is demonstrated how easily a parent can injure a child's psychological development by not being aware of the tremendous influence parents have on their children. The parent believes he is teaching his son life lessons. Instead, he is influencing him to overinflate his ego with winning—and to lie and cheat if you cannot win.

Winning is the goal in this scenario. None of the principles of karate are applied here. One of the saddest trends I see in my practice with young adolescents is that the art of thinking is not encouraged. Children are forced into activities and live scheduled lives. They have fun, but no one is asking if they had fun at the game, karate school, or other activities.

Children have access to technology and information instantly, and it seems to impede their ability to think. Learning to think abstractly is a developmental task that occurs in adolescence. Thinking involves processing information and learning how to make decisions and cope with emotions. A major part of helping children's cognitive development comes from communicating with them about their activities and emotions.

In this situation, we do not have enough information to know if Gary wanted to spar with Master Paul or show off his interest in wrestling. It appears that his father wanted him to participate and spoke directly to Master Paul about challenging his son. However, this experience will remain with Gary as he enters adulthood. I would guess that there is no clarity in his mind about this situation.

If parents communicate with their children and listen, the children learn valuable life skills, decision-making, emotional regulation, and healthy creativity to explore other interests. This situation reminds me of many clinical stories where a child is reaching for something, perhaps a new interest in wrestling, and the desire gets derailed and misunderstood with a parent's agenda.

I want to encourage parents to have aspirations for their children within their capacities and interests. Parents have tremendous influence on their children for a short time. That influence remains with a child, and I encourage parents to treat that influence with integrity and respect.

Tsabary, Shefali, *The Conscious Parent*, Namaste Publishing, (2010).

Exam Week

> He that is good making excuses is seldom good for anything else.
> —Benjamin Franklin

Exciting and energetic classes lead to attendance. Attendance leads to progress, and progress leads to exams. Growth and progress are one of the six human needs. We all need to see and feel growth. It's one of those universal truths. That which does not grow dies. Testing in the martial arts is a great way for students to challenge themselves and set and achieve short and long-term goals.

All schools conduct tests in their own ways. I test at my schools every six weeks. Not every student tests. They have to qualify, take a certain number of classes, and pretest or quiz on the required curriculum. If they pass the pretest, then they can take the exam. They must have their classes, pass the pretest, and go forward. Simple. If they can't perform the material, they can't move forward. If you can't add and subtract, you can't go to second grade.

It's a fairly simple system with checks and balances to ensure a standard. Why test a student who's not prepared? Students know when exam day is. Prior to exam day, there is a pretest week and a review week. Some parents want their children to advance when they're not prepared or ready to test.

Every six weeks or so, some parents gets their noses out of joint. Some parents feel like they know more than the instructors—and the child should test because "it's been so long since Johnny tested." It is usually more about the parent trying to keep up with the neighbor's kid or other parents in the lobby who are going on and on about how their children are head and shoulders above the rest. It's a whole keeping up with the Joneses thing.

The belts are nothing more than a goal system. Back in the day, there were no colored belts. The person with the dirtiest, most tattered belt was the most experienced. The person with the cleanest belt—the belt that looked new and unused—was the beginner. You advanced through class attendance and proficiency in the material. You never asked to be tested. Asking the instructor to test before he asked you was considered disrespectful and in poor taste.

When you were asked to test, there were no curriculums, review weeks, and written materials. You were told you would be tested, and you were to perform material from class. We did it, and we advanced. All of our psyches remained intact. It's a little different today.

Zack was a brown belt. At that level, students must pretest on the prior belt ranks (beginner through advanced material). The brown belts can test every cycle if they choose to. Since it's a review, they have already tested on this material. All they have to do is ask for the paperwork to test and submit it to their instructors. The paperwork is a permission to test application that the parents and teachers fill out prior to the exam. The simple form asks if the candidate is showing respect, using manners at home, and passing in school.

Zack and his mother could never do that. Every time there was testing, there would be a problem. Zack forgot to ask, or his mom forgot to ask. The paperwork was lost. It wasn't a big deal. We still tested Zack—with the condition that it was his responsibility. After five years of training, there comes a time to stand up and be confident, responsible, and accountable for one's actions. Rank imposes responsibility—not privilege. That was the lesson we tried to instill.

Another testing approached, and Zack was unprepared. After several free private lessons, Zack and his mom couldn't communicate—or maybe they didn't think the rules applied to him. The instructor decided Zack was not prepared and had not submitted the exam notice in a timely fashion. He would have to wait another six weeks. The mom began to huff and puff at the front desk and made a scene about how it was "bullshit." She grabbed her son and abruptly left the school.

She was bad-mouthing the instructors and the school to any parent who was there. What a shame. He was months away from testing for a black belt. Who was she hurting? He would have to be responsible one day for work deadlines, college applications, loan applications, and schoolwork. Why do parents insulate their children from being accountable and responsible? Why is that a bad thing?

The following week, I received a letter that Zack and his family were quitting. It made no sense to me. Some people feel a sense of entitlement and don't think rules and policies apply to them. Isn't it our job as parents to teach and guide our children? Exam week does bring out some small and petty-minded thinking. Exams are supposed to test, challenge, encourage, and reward those who have made efforts and improvements. We see entitlement issues too often in life. People do the bare minimum and expect huge rewards.

Mr. Black couldn't afford for all four of his children to learn martial arts, but he let me know that the police department referred him. He was in law enforcement and had heard of me. He wanted them to train at my school. I helped him out financially and only charged for two kids. All four children came for the price of two. We always had a good relationship. He would make friendly conversation and tell me about the latest news in the police world—and how much he was bench-pressing at the gym. One time, he even invited himself over to my home so he could see my new kitchen. He wanted to get some ideas.

I thought we had a good relationship. For four years, I had never had a cross word with the parents, and the children had good attendance. They were above-average students and came to most of the events we hosted at the school.

During exam week, all four kids were testing. They went through the normal procedures. They passed the pretests, but the youngest daughter had a little trouble with some of the material. She was instructed about what to practice to have a stronger test.

This exam day was great. Every session was awesome. The students were prepared, full of energy, and had winning attitudes. They felt they could conquer the world. The school was buzzing with that attitude, and the students were feeding off of it. The kicks were sharp, the punches were strong, and the throws and takedowns were on point. It was a great testing day until the youngest member of the Black family's turn.

She forgot or didn't perform anything that was asked of her. The rest of the Black kids were on point and prepared. The youngest was lost in the sauce. When I asked her to go right, she went left. If I asked her to perform a Kata, she stared at me. When I asked for kick, I got a punch. It was bad. I asked, "Are you okay? Are you scared?"

She said, "I'm fine."

I asked, "Did you practice for today's test?"

"No, I was at a sleepover last night, and we didn't sleep."

I hated to do it, but since she didn't meet the standard and admitted she was not prepared, she would have to fail the exam and retake the test in six weeks.

When her mom and dad came to pick up the children, I explained what had happened. I could see they were disappointed that their youngest had failed her exam. I offered additional help with private lessons, and they said they had another party to go to.

Three days later, I ran into Mr. Black at the gym. I had seen him there on several occasions, and our relationship had always been good. Instead of telling me how much he was bench-pressing, how far he had run on the treadmill, or body-fat ratio, he said "The kids are done."

"The kids are done?"

"Yeah. They're not coming back. We talked about it, and if one of us fails, we all fail."

I almost fell off the weight bench. "So, because your daughter failed, everyone is leaving?"

"Yeah—unless you want to reconsider your decision and pass her."

I couldn't have been more surprised if he had hit me in the face with a bucket of ice water. "Your daughter was not prepared. She didn't do the work. She admitted that she didn't do the work. I can't pass her just because her brothers and sisters passed."

"Well, we are all in this together. That's our decision." The big, bad law enforcement official who valued hard work, my credentials, my school's track record, and its reputation for producing quality students was taking his four kids out because one did not meet the requirements. And he wanted me to change my decision in order to keep them at the school?

I said, "See ya."

It only devalues the rank promotion for everyone who has earned it if we promote those who don't deserve it. Why do parents feel that when a child fails at something, it is a life-threatening event? Sometimes you win, and sometimes you learn. I have failed or lost many times, and those failures and losses helped me to become the man I am today. Winston Churchill said, "The price for greatness is responsibility." Let's teach our children to welcome failure as a resource to tap into. Every swing of the bat brings me closer to a home run.

Failure can teach you a tremendous amount. Successful people don't quit. I've known many people who have been knocked down, failed, and been on the losing side once, twice, or dozens of times. Successful people have the ability to bounce back. They have a very short downtime. They recover quickly. They pick themselves up, dust themselves off, and continue toward their goals. They do not wallow in pity because they know nothing good comes from it.

Clinical Wisdom from Carol Davis, LCSW

> You cannot help people permanently by doing for them,
> what they could and should do for themselves.
> —Abraham Lincoln

There is great wisdom in these words, yet parents are and living vicariously through the successes and failures of their children. I am not sure why everyone has to win and why parents are insisting on this message for their children. Folks learn so much through failure and not winning. The simple task of reflecting on your behavior seems lost in this culture of entitlement.

Parents enroll children in martial arts for a multitude of reasons. If a child is shy and socially awkward, martial arts can bolster self-esteem and teach a child the principles behind martial arts. Some children exhibit attention deficit problems or are overly aggressive. Learning martial arts can help teach respect, courtesy, integrity, perseverance, and self-control while fostering an indomitable spirit. What parent is opposed to children developing these qualities? The philosophy is positive and helpful to many young people. Over time, parents begin to see changes in their children as they master the art.

If I could speak to the parents these situations, I would ask them to explain their plans and hopes for their children. As Abraham Lincoln said so brilliantly, it is a disservice to children to cover up or rescue them from situations they could learn from. By standing up for yourself, you learn a valuable life lesson. Children who expect everything to go their ways grow up to be narcissistic adults or self-centered people who lack ambition, empathy, and creativity.

Amy McCready is nationally known parenting expert who wrote The "Me, Me, Me" Epidemic: A Step-by-Step Guide to Raising Capable, Grateful Kids in an Over-Entitled World. She says parents need to stop negotiating with their children for their needs and give them what is needed. Children need attention, consistency, chores, responsibility, and discipline, but they also need your time—and they need to be listened to.

In my practice, I have seen numerous young people who literally have no opinions and have not developed the skill of thinking on their own. Everything they do requires approval and validation. I'm treating a young college student who cannot decide what to hang in her dorm room without checking with her mother for approval and validation. She has lived an indulged life, and at the age of nineteen, she cannot make any decisions without her mother. Of course, part of the treatment is working with the mother to detach and allow her daughter to emancipate and learn coping and decision-making. Her first year in college was full of panic and anxiety because she was away from her mother.

I cannot stress enough the importance of children finding their voices and making decisions. Entitlement, in psychological terms, is inherently a healthy, desired feeling. It is the feeling that you are capable and allowed to pursue the things you want to do. Egotism demands that all experiences go your way and that one should have anything and everything one wants.

True entitlement is a gift: feeling capable and allowed to pursue and allowing an individual to develop self-respect and dignity. This process instills confidence and respect for self and others. In our society, this basic human need has exploded into a state where parents and children engage in fights over what is owed to them—a certificate in karate, a pass in an exam, or an iPad. Instead of assessing what interfered with passing the exam, the child is withdrawn from the program.

My concern is that many decisions are made without considering the child's input. The long-range effects can lead to children becoming young adults with no voices or "learned narcissism." Children are precious. As parents, we have to take the time to teach them with loving-kindness and set boundaries in our children's lives. What is there to be learned from having to take the exam later? The answer offers endless possibilities for a child's development.

McCready, Amy, *The Me, Me, Me Epidemic: A Step-by-Step Guide to Raising Capable, Grateful Kids in an Over-Entitled World*, (2016).

It's none of your business.

I use a little poem about telling the truth and the importance of honesty.

> Tell the truth and tell it ever
> Costeth what it will,
> For he who hides the wrong he did
> Does the wrong thing still.
> —Zig Ziglar's mother

When mothers and fathers enroll their children in my school, they aren't completely forthcoming about their children's preexisting conditions. Some children have allergies, autism, serious medical conditions like rheumatoid arthritis, diabetes, and asthma, and neurological conditions that make it difficult for the children to process information.

When we know the whole story, it makes the learning and teaching experience a bit easier, which benefits the students. It's all about service. It we don't know, we can't serve the students properly.

Experience is the best teacher. After many years of teaching and serving the public, I have the ability to see what's going on with most students who come in for lessons. There are signs in their body language, their eyes, and their speech. We know something is going on with the child, but without a parent's confirmation, it's just speculation.

I always wondered why parents would choose not to inform teachers, instructors, aides, or anyone else in a position of influencing their children about any condition that might hinder them. Wouldn't you want to disclose those things if it would help your child progress?

Dylan was an excellent student with great attendance. He was a fine athlete who picked up the class material quickly. His parents were a bit standoffish. Always on the go, they were the quintessential example of the "drop-and-go" parent. They would dump the kid off at class and never come inside the building. They never knew what was going on in the school and never knew when the events were happening. They were disconnected from the school and what their son was doing. It was sad, especially because Dylan really strived. He made great progress and was headed for success in the martial arts.

Dylan had reached the level where he was able to spar (Kumite). The standard protective equipment included a head protector, hand and foot pads, a mouthpiece, and a groin protector. Dylan's mom actually went inside the school to purchase the equipment. At first I didn't know who she was because I rarely saw her.

She inquired about how sparring worked and how hard a student could get hit. I explained sparring and the light contact that is involved. She understood, thanked me for my time, and left after purchasing the equipment.

Dylan was a natural at sparring and really picked it up fast. He could kick and punch and throw combinations at his opponents. He would even fake a technique and then score with another technique.

For a few months, Dylan kept improving. His parents never saw him in action. They were never there. I'm sure they had a lot going on with work and other children, but it would have been nice for Dylan if they made the time to see him.

Children don't remember how much money you spend on them, but they remember how much time you spend with them.

Dylan eventually received his green belt (a midlevel rank). He had between eighteen and twenty-four months of experience.

His mother came in after he was promoted to green belt. She was her normal self—all business, few words, cold, and distant. She handed me a very professional-looking envelope from the Children's Hospital of Philadelphia. "Dylan's done with karate."

"Oh my gosh. Is everything okay?" I asked.

"He's fine, but his doctor thought it would be best for him not to do this anymore."

"His doctor?"

Dylan's doctor thought it would be in his best interests not to continue with karate because of his hemophilia. Dylan had been a hemophiliac since he was a baby.

I was not exactly sure what hemophilia was, but it didn't sound very good. I said that I was sorry to lose Dylan from the program, and I thanked her for her support and loyalty. I told her I hoped our paths would cross in the future.

She reminded me that they still had a class or two coming to them and would be in one last time. She didn't want to miss out on what she had paid for.

"Are you sure?" I asked.

"Yes," she said. "See you tomorrow."

"But what about the doctor?"

"It will be okay," she said.

Later that day, I had a private lesson with a pediatrician who had been a student and friend of mine for years. As we were preparing for our weekly lesson, I told him about a student of mine who had to quit because he had hemophilia. "Hey, Doc. What is that anyway?"

His face said it all. "There's a child here training with hemophilia?"

"Yes."

"Master Paul, maybe you heard her wrong?"

"No," I said. I explained the letter from the doctor.

He informed me to get the boy out of the school. "He could die. You could kill him. He could bleed internally if he gets hit. How long has he been in class?"

"Almost two years," I replied.

The pediatrician was dumbfounded. He could not believe this boy had been training in the martial arts for almost two years and had been treated for hemophilia. He couldn't believe that the parents would allow it since there was a risk of contact. The Mayo Clinic said this about hemophilia:

> Hemophilia is a rare disorder in which your blood doesn't clot normally because it lacks sufficient blood-clotting proteins (clotting factors). If you have hemophilia, you may bleed for a longer time after an injury than you would if your blood clotted normally.
>
> Small cuts usually aren't much of a problem. The greater health concern is deep bleeding inside your body, especially in your knees, ankles and elbows. That internal bleeding can damage your organs and tissues, and may be life-threatening.

After getting an earful of information, I was pissed. Why had she put her son in harm's way? Why had she put me—and my business—at risk? Why hadn't she informed me? Why not disclose his medical history? One of the first things we inquire about when a student comes into the school is a medical history. I was so pissed—and I was really looking forward to seeing the mother.

She walked into the school the next day, and I stopped her in her tracks. I informed her that Dylan couldn't take the class. I told her I'd consulted with some medical professionals and decided it was best not to run that risk any further. "Your son has hemophilia, a serious and life-threatening disease. He could have gotten hurt. I could've hurt him without knowing. Why didn't you say something sooner?"

"It was none of your business," she said.

"None of my business? You put me—and my staff and business—at risk."

She made a face and left. She had endangered her child because she didn't know how to communicate. She'd put her child at risk. How weak and selfish can one be? She would constantly drop her child off—a child with hemophilia—and just leave. Who does that?

The staff had no clue about the boy's medical problem. What if something had happened? Was she so afraid of labeling her child that she risked his health and safety?

Clinical Wisdom from Carol Davis, LCSW

When a child is diagnosed with an illness or a disability, it is a difficult task for the parents to accept that their child will have a different life. Professionals will often assess that a parent is in denial, and perhaps the term needs to be reframed when it comes to childhood illness and disabilities.

Many years ago, Helen Keller's mother refused to place her in an asylum. She was determined to find a solution for her daughter. Her determination and spirit of optimism prevailed despite the hardships, leaving Helen Keller with the ability to communicate. Parents face this with illness; they often act with hope and high expectations. They want to treat their children like other children. With advances in technology and medical science, no one can accurately predict what children with illnesses and disabilities are capable of. There are so many factors to consider in diagnosing a child, and it is often a lengthy process. In this situation, I am going to be the optimist and assume that the mother, although disengaged, may not have understood the full range of his disorder.

There has been debate in the literature about whether parents are going through a grief process or an adaptation process. Family members process information in different stages and often at different times. In 1969, Elisabeth Kubler-Ross presented us with a grief model consisting of denial, grief, despair, anger, and acceptance. In 1994, Miller interviewed parents of disabled children and explained how parents process information within an adaptation model. The four elements of the adaptation model are surviving, searching, settling in, and separating. This model suggests a circular process with a dynamic quality due to the child and the family needing to find meaning in their lives. When you live with someone with a disability or an illness that limits him or her, multiple transitions will occur.

I urge parents to look beyond the grief model and have hopes for their children—even if they are different hopes. Parents experience a range of emotions at different intervals in their children's lives. I would guess that this encounter with Master Paul was one of those transitional periods. As difficult as it was for Master Paul to hear about this child's hemophilia, it is unclear what stage of the diagnosis the child was in when he entered the karate school. There is no task more difficult than taking a loved hobby or sport away from a child. Dylan was excelling and loving karate, and he had to stop. Perhaps the mother was in a transitional space and was adapting to his illness. She might have been searching for an explanation to give Master Paul.

Call me an optimist, but it's difficult to judge families with chronic illness. My husband was disabled. He was not a child, but we moved through many transitions (from walking to a motorized wheelchair). We were often met with bewilderment and misunderstandings from providers and society when he would attempt to accomplish something that was "out of reach for a disabled person."

People require time to process unexpected news about the health of their children. There are times when parents "act normal" with their children or push the pause button as they cope with devastating news that requires change and interventions. I would venture to guess that this was one of those moments in this family's life.

When a child is enrolling in a program, it is crucial to provide accurate health information. This situation requires compassion and understanding since the family is dealing with an illness. Given the research done in this area and in my experience, I would offer the following suggestions for coaches, teachers, and parents:

- Support parents' hopes and dreams for their children.
- Suspend judgment of families and their behaviors.
- Be patient. People need time to find their own ways with illness and disability.
- View it as an opportunity to build trust.
- Educate others to rethink denial when it comes to children and disability.
- Encourage honesty and openness.

Parents facing life-changing disorders need to be given compassion. This is not to suggest that Master Paul was acting in a judgmental way. As an optimist, I am suggesting that he was presented with the news in a shocking, abrupt way, which may illustrate how families experience difficult information. In situations like this, we need to realize the complexity of coping with childhood illnesses and disabilities.

Miller, Mark et al, "Applying Interpersonal Psychotherapy to Bereavement-Related Depression Following Loss of Spouse in Late Life," *The Journal of Psychotherapy Practice and Research*, (1994).

Denial ain't a river in Egypt.

Our culture has taken a hard turn in a direction that doesn't help our children. We text when we should call and communicate. We e-mail because we don't want to talk or have face-to-face interaction. We take selfies of the car crash before helping the victims and reward children for poor behavior, bad manners, and disrespect.

What gives? "He's so smart. He can recite all the presidents—and do it backward too." That's a weak mom who's in denial. Dominic was a lot of work from the time he entered the school until the time he left. It was my suspicion that he had some type of oppositional defiant disorder—or maybe was on the spectrum of autism. Either way, he was rude and disrespectful to adults and children. He needed correction, rules, boundaries, and respect for people and property. Dominic wasn't getting any of the latter at home.

Dominic had a habit of frequently interrupting conversations (like most children do from time to time), calling out in class while others were speaking, and smacking his legs and feet while sitting and standing. He thought he was the teacher—and that it was his responsibility to correct the instructors and his classmates. He didn't know his rank in the pack.

When we would ask his mother why he smacked his legs and feet, they said, "He does that when he's excited."

His progress report from school said he wouldn't do this or that, he wanted to be away from the other children, and he wanted to be alone at his own table. He was disrespectful to others.

I asked, "What's going on?"

His mother would say, "He's just so smart," "He's bored," or "He needs to be challenged more." I understand that smart, gifted children with high IQs need to be challenged more in school. Why are they allowed to be rude and disrespectful? Do the parents really think that correcting them and holding them accountable will damage their psyches or inhibit their future selves? Will we stop their creative juices and stymie any pending intellect?

Dominic had to be reminded at all times that he wasn't in charge, that there were other children in the class, and that it wasn't all about him. We are a group. We are a class. We are a family. We are a team. We are a school. We are a society.

Dominic and his mother had a tough time grasping those concepts.

I said, "Is there anything I need to know? Are there any medical issues I should be aware of?"

"Nope," she said.

When we had to correct him or have a chat about Dominic's behavior, she would giggle at him and his answers for why he spit on someone, talked backed to an instructor, or hit, pushed, shoved, or cursed at another student. It was cute to her, and it was excusable to her because he got straight As.

Awesome! He has straight As, but he can't say hello and good-bye. He can't say please and thank you, and he has no friends. I'm happy I got Bs and Cs in school. I'm ecstatic that my daughter has a 3.5 GPA. In Dominic's defense, he can recite all the presidents' names—and do it backward.

Dominic's mother was upset because Dominic's teachers felt he needed to be "classified." The teachers felt that he should be evaluated. Dominic exhibited behaviors of Asperger's syndrome, which is an autism spectrum disorder (ASD) that is characterized by significant difficulties in social interaction and nonverbal communication, alongside restricted and repetitive patterns of behavior and interests.

The mom was terrified that her son would be "labeled" and put into another class. I felt empathy for mom and Dominic, but are we serving him if we do not know how to help, treat, teach, reach, instruct, and guide him?

Denial is not a river in Egypt. My suspicions were correct. I think the mom knew it the entire time, but she did not want to confront it. She needed to get out of her own way, and she did when her son had a meltdown in class. He ran to the bathroom, locked himself inside, and wouldn't come out for almost an hour. If we picked the lock, he would hold his finger on the lock to prevent us from opening it. When he came out, he didn't recite the president's names for me.

After a few months, they left. Before they left, the mom told me her son was seeing a therapist and was being treated for Asperger's. I wish she had been more forthcoming from the very beginning.

Clinical Wisdom from Carol Davis, LCSW

> Nothing is to be clung to as I, me, or mine. In other words, no attachments—especially to fixed ideas of yourself and who you are.
> —Jon Kabat-Zinn

Compassion has been lost in this culture. We rush from one activity to another, trying to handle life's trials and tribulations. In its basic form, it means applying the Golden Rule to our lives.

"Love your neighbor as yourself." Most people can relate to this phrase, but it is difficult to practice for a mother who is dealing with a challenging child with multiple behavioral issues and intellectual superiority. This mother was attached to the notion that her son was highly intelligent, which was true. However, massive behavior signs and symptoms were being ignored probably because it is painful to admit and accept an unknown path for a child.

Many parents lose touch with the need for love and understanding. It requires taking the time to pause, observe, and possibly describe a child's situation without judgment or jealousy. Some parents are so involved in loving and caring for their children that they lose sight of their own needs. It can be a problem for the children if the parents don't care for themselves psychologically. This woman was so involved in protecting her son's intellectual mind that she neglected herself and her child.

If I was a therapist in Master Paul's school and had the opportunity to interact with Dominic's mom, I would say, "Can we sit and talk?"

I would ask questions about her experiences in school and why she thinks being smart is more important than respect and cooperation. There is more than likely a link to her attachment to his IQ. Needless to say, this woman is suffering with her child—and the child is being misread and is not receiving psychological treatment.

I cannot stress enough the importance of early intervention with children on the autism spectrum. It is equally wise for parents to engage in therapy to further understand their children, discuss their emotions, and develop compassion and empathy for themselves in living with autism disorders. Parents often ignore the signs and symptoms because they blame themselves or think something went wrong in their parenting. Being attached to an idea, as Jon Kabat-Zinn writes in his quote, can lead to unhealthy living. There are so many options to help people cope with life's trials. Psychotherapy, meditation, yoga, and other holistic modalities can help a person manage life.

In my years as a therapist, the primary obstacle to treating ourselves with compassion is that most folks are addicted to self-criticism. It starts early in life, and other obstacles—abuse, neglect, physical illness, psychological distress, or learning disorders—make the journey more difficult in our fast-paced society. The mom may feel alone in her struggles. When this occurs, people tend to use denial as a defense mechanism. I suspect there is an inner critic within this mom—and I would try to help her release that inner critic through therapy.

Perel, Esther, *Mating in Captivity*, Harper Collins Publishers, (2006).

4

Respect

I won't be wronged. I won't be insulted. I won't
be laid a-hand on. I don't do these things to other
people, and I require the same from them.
—John Wayne, The Shootist

Rendezvous by the Dumpster

Owning a martial arts school is gratifying in many
ways. You get to meet fantastic children and parents,
and you get to make an impression on the youth of
America. You have the opportunity to build a strong
community—one child at a time. You're respected, you're in a position
of authority, and you make a great wage.

When you work with the public, you meet all sorts of people.
I've met people who held positions in Fortune 500 companies and
musicians who played with Frankie Valli, the Four Seasons, and Ed
Sullivan. One parent was a former Franciscan monk. It was a true
melting pot of diversity.

The former monk was a kind, gentle, respectful, and peace-loving
man. He was a wonderful father and husband and a great supporter
of the school. I've never heard a bad word come out of his mouth.

He said, "Two mothers are making out behind the building by the garbage Dumpster. I thought you might want to know—in case the kids happen to be back there."

"What?" I said. "No. You're mistaken."

"Master Paul, I know what making out looks like, and I thought you should know."

Were they were so happy to throw out their garbage that they decided to hug? Were they consoling themselves over garbage that was already thrown out? Was the former monk telling tales because he wanted to stir the pot and cause trouble? I opted to mind my own business because it was outside the school, no one was around, and no kids were involved,

I decided to keep it to myself. What else could I do? They weren't hurting anybody. Dawn was right about 98 percent of the time. She had a great gift for reading people. She could have been an FBI profiler in another life. She told me the moms were trouble. She mentioned that she always saw them together and never one without the other.

They would drop the kids off at different karate classes because they had to do something. If people wanted more of what I was doing, it could lead to more business. I was new, and I never questioned it. Dawn knew something was going on between them.

On testing day, we set up chairs around the perimeter of the dojo. The students sit with legs crossed, chests out, shoulders back, and heads up. This formal sitting position shows discipline, focus, and presence. The first time I allowed spectators, I was bit nervous. I was extra cautious with my paperwork and made sure I had the correct number of belts and diplomas. There is nothing worse than forgetting to give a child a belt and diploma at a graduation in front of the parents.

As I was checking my paperwork and belts for the fiftieth time in my closet-sized office, I could feel the tension. The nervous students had lined up like soldiers.

One of the moms yelled, "You bitch. I fucking love you. You broke my heart. How can you do this? I fucking love you."

The other mom was sitting angelically with her husband.

I nearly soiled myself. When I opened my door, the mom was yelling in front of twenty-five children and at least twenty-five parents and family members.

The mother with her husband held his hand and said, "What's going on? Who are you? Why are you saying these things to me?" She didn't even flinch. She stuck to her script and never wavered. It was a great performance.

I grabbed the heartbroken mother who was yelling and crying. I felt sorry for her. She was hyperventilating, and snot was coming out of her nose.

As I escorted her out of the school, the woman's father came up to me. He had not said two words to me in two years. He said, "Paul, I'm sorry. They love each other. They've been together for a while now and—"

I said, "Please leave. We can discuss this at another time."

I had to focus on the children who were testing. The poor kids had witnessed two adult moms having a heated lovers' spat with f-bombs flying all over the room. I conducted the test, and the kids did what they were supposed to do. It should have been a happy day for all of those who were there, but it was tainted by the nonsense of those moms.

Later that week, I spoke to the mother who started the drama. She apologized to me and started to tell me about their relationship.

I said, "That's not my business. I don't want to know about your relationship. I don't appreciate you two bringing your crap into my business. I think it would be best if you just dropped your son off at the front door. He is welcome to continue taking classes, but I don't want to see you in my school for the next thirty days."

She understood she had screwed up, and she was sorry. She accepted the penalty and adhered to it.

The other mom was not going to go quietly. She was the victim. She had no idea why that woman spoke to her that way. And her husband had absolutely no idea. He was totally clueless, and I was the one who was supposed to tell him? Part of me just wanted to slam her and tell her husband what I knew. I thought it would be more professional if I kept my mouth closed and just administered the same penalty to her. I was going to use a zero-tolerance policy.

When I met with this mom and her husband, she was still playing the victim. She was holding her husband's hand and said, "This town is full of crazies. You know, Paul?"

I bit my tongue and didn't engage. I said, "That was an unfortunate incident. It should never have happened—and it definitely should not have been witnessed by the children and their families." I explained that her son was welcome to take class, but it would be best if she dropped her son off at the front door and picked him up after class for the next thirty days.

They were utterly astonished. They stood there as if I had thrown a bucket of ice water in their faces. She started to cry. She had no idea why I was doing this. "I was the victim," she wailed.

The husband said, "Why are you doing this to us, Paul? We were the victims. She approached us. We never said a word." He had no clue, and I didn't want to be the one to tell him.

I said, "This is my decision. Please respect it."

The husband, a local businessman, tried several times to sway me. He said he understood, but he stuck to his position. After his wife stormed out, he asked if I would reconsider because he would hate to leave and involve his lawyer.

A big smile appeared on my face. "Well, you can do whatever you want, but this is a private school. I don't have to tolerate nonsense like that. For the record, sir, I don't think you have all the facts. You might want to sit down with your wife and talk to her about what really happened." At that point, my patience was out the window.

For the next thirty days, phone calls and letters asked me to make an exception and reverse my decision.

I stuck to my guns.

The kids came to class, worked hard, and did what they were supposed to do. They learned, had fun, and rose in the ranks. It was crazy, but it was my fault. I should've ended everything that day and exposed her for what she was: a liar, a cheat, and a selfish person who cared about nothing but herself.

Everything cooled down after thirty days. I think the father realized that his son was benefitting from the program. As far as I know, the moms were never an item again. I never had another cross word with either one. They continued to come to the school. Their children went on to higher ranks, and one even made it to black belt.

After both families left the school, I learned that the mom who played the victim left her husband for another man and moved to another state.

When a former monk tells you something, you shouldn't doubt him.

Clinical Wisdom from Carol Davis, LCSW

We live in an era where we feel that we are entitled to pursue our desires, because this is the culture where I deserve to be happy. And if we used to divorce because we were unhappy, today we divorce because we could be happier. And if divorce carried all the shame, today, choosing to stay when you can leave is the new shame.
—Esther Perel, Mating in Captivity

In my clinical practice providing individual, marital, and family therapy, I have experienced the gamut of experiences not unlike the experience at the Dumpster. We live in a world of great entitlement to being happy. As Americans, we believe it is our right—and we strive for to remain happy. This sets up many problems for individuals and families since it is an impossible goal.

Esther Perel discusses the struggles of married folks in Mating in Captivity. She informs us of the perils couples face and how the perils impact children. An affair is an emotional crisis for a couple and the family. The situation at the Dumpster presents as a challenge to Master Paul, the children, and the school.

One might ask, "What's the problem? They aren't hurting anyone."

I would disagree with this premise. I have worked with children and families who are confused by emotional and physical affairs. The scars may be invisible. Many children attend karate school to gain inner strength for self-esteem, develop a secure self-trust that can be internalized into personality development, and obtain mastery of physical and mental challenges. Some parents assume their children will not be harmed and operate on the premise that kids are resilient.

Regardless of their ages, children know when something is amiss with their parents—and infidelity raises the insecurity bar. Research on the impact of infidelity reveals that children are faced with intense anger, anxiety, guilt, shame, sadness, and confusion. Many children withdraw, regress, act out, and assume the role of caregiver for the injured parent.

When a parent participates in infidelity, children can intuitively sense that something has changed in their parents' relationship. It could be the tone of voice or the absence of seeing them together. I have seen couples move out of the bedroom, sleep in another room, and not consider the child's perception of this major change. Children often view this disruption as a betrayal. They often experience feelings of inadequacy and emotional pain that leave them helpless to express their emotions because their security has been jeopardized. Infidelity can trigger regressive behavior in their emotional, intellectual, and physical lives. The effects can remain buried within a child until they begin to engage in interpersonal relationships. It can manifest as a fear or belief that it is impossible to trust anyone.

Marriages do not always last however, and it is important to consider the impact of your decisions on your children's lives. Children can thrive despite the struggles if their needs are considered. It takes a child time to adjust to a parent loving someone else, and it is optimal if parents provide time to a child.

I cannot emphasize enough the importance of communication with children. If there is no language associated with experiences that are not understandable to a child, the child is left to imagination and an inner voice that often turns critical toward the child because the child is sad. A sad mood in a child without language can lead to childhood depression or concentration problems in school. Children also learn that lying is normal, and denial becomes part of their coping skills.

In my experience, one of the most difficult aspects of depression, especially with children, is the presence of a negative inner critic that can become a lifelong companion. I urge parents to communicate the changes in their lives with their children. It is essential that you are ready to begin this discussion. This discussion is for the children and is not a way to talk about your spouse to your children. Respecting their love for the other parent will manifest in a positive direction for all involved. There are games and books for children that will assist them in accepting an aspect of life that may be difficult (a separation, new relationship, or divorce).

Resources for Parents

The Helping, Sharing, and Caring Workbook by Lisa M. Schab, LCSW, with Richard A. Gardner, MD

Active Parenting of Teens: Parent's Guide by Michael H. Popkin, PhD

The Parent's Handbook by Don Dinkmeyer Sr., Gary D. McKay, and Don Dinkmeyer Jr.

Tricks of the Trade: 101 Psychological Techniques to Help Children Grow and Change by Lawrence Shapiro, PhD

The Scoop on Infidelity by Ester Perel

Infidelity: The Lessons Children Learn by Jennifer Harley Chalmers, PhD

The Impact of Adult Infidelity on Children by Dr. Ana Nogales

Diagnostic and Statistical Manual of Mental Disorders, Fifth Edition American Psychiatric Association, (2013).

Baby Food

Throughout the years, I have witnessed a lot of scary family rituals and routines. Some parents need to be slapped—and slapped hard and continuously. These parents need to be slapped with weighted gloves. Then after they are slapped, they need to be enrolled at the local charm and etiquette school.

When Mrs. Wilkes came in to enroll her son—who had multiple behavior problems—she let us know that her kid was "a bastard like his father." She let us know this tasty nugget of information in front of her child.

Her eight-year-old son had attention deficit disorder, hyperactivity, and obsessive-defiant disorder. He did not listen at home or at school, and he fought with his brother and sister. We definitely had our work cut out for us.

Master Dave handled the evaluation lesson. The boy performed the material asked of him, was polite and mannerly, listened to instructions, and tried his best. He showed all the signs of a student who wanted to be at the school. The mom liked what she saw and signed him up for the six-week trial program. If I knew then what I know now, I would have handed back her money. The boy had far deeper problems.

The first six weeks weren't that bad. We were basically teaching the student how to be a student. The boy was a little lost at times, forgot some rules, and learned what would be tolerated (and what wouldn't).

The mom thought karate was a magic pill. She thought karate would transform her boy from what she and her husband had created. I've read that a person's personality and behaviors come from 70 percent environment and 30 percent genes. That would explain a lot.

After six weeks, Mrs. Wilkes renewed her program. I guess she was starting to see some improvement with her son at home. If parents follow our lead, do what we do at home, and be consistent with praise and corrections, they will see progress in their child. There has to be consistency, and everyone has to be on the same page.

The Wilkes boy was transforming—but only when he was in the karate school. When he left, that's when the shit hit the fan.

At the next class, the mom approached an instructor, handed off her son, and said, "He's cursing at me

"He's cursing at you? You're cursing at your mother?"

The boy stared at me and batted his eyes.

The mom said, "He told me to go fuck myself."

I told the mother of the year to lower her voice because there were young children present. "I heard you the first time," I said.

I let the boy know how awful it was to talk to his mother like that.

He apologized to us and promised never to do it again.

Why did it happen? It was over baby food. The mom fed her eight-year-old son baby food. He didn't like the baby food she was feeding him. I guess she bought the wrong brand of strained bananas, and he went off on her.

"Why was your son eating baby food?"

"He has swallowing issues."

"Oh, okay. Does he have an injury or ailment I should know about?"

"No," she said. "He won't eat anything else."

I'm no doctor, but it sounded very strange. It seemed there was another problem, but no one was offering up any information.

The dad wasn't much help. When he would come in, all he could talk about was how his kid was screwing up, that Krav Maga (an Israeli self-defense system) was the best martial art, and that this stuff was a joke. He was always insulting and condescending to the staff and to his own family. I agreed with his wife. He was a low-class, ignorant bastard.

That was the routine. The mom would come in, grab an instructor, and talk about of her son. He was cursing her out, fighting, arguing, and having eating problems. We would counsel the boy and give him progress reports to be filled out by his parents. We tried to make him accountable for his actions at home. It never happened. The progress reports were always lost or incomplete. When the boy bit another kid at our Halloween party, his father said, "Boys will be boys." No wonder the child had problems.

After a few months she said, "This karate thing ain't working."

"The karate thing isn't working?" I said. "Where's the dad in all this? What does he do when your son acts this way at home?"

"He's a fucking idiot. He's an old Italian. He doesn't care. He just wants his dinner on the table."

I knew I was in over my head when she told me her son was choking and beating the family dog.

I said, "Sounds like your son needs therapy. Is he seeing anyone now?"

"Yeah. He's seeing some Jew guy."

"Some Jew guy?"

I canceled their program and wished them well. I also informed her that if her child was harming the family pet that she needed to address it immediately with a psychiatric professional.

It's tragic when parents are indifferent and disconnected from their children. With parenting like that, the boy's future was grim.

Psychology Today
Children Who are Cruel to Animals: When to Worry
Childhood animal cruelty can be normal or a red flag.
Post published by Joni E Johnston PsyD on Apr 27,
2011, in The Human Equation

Since the 1970s, research has consistently reported
childhood cruelty to animals as the first warning sign
of later delinquency, violence, and criminal behavior.
In fact, nearly all violent crime perpetrators have a
history of animal cruelty in their profiles. Albert
deSalvo, the Boston Strangler found guilty of killing
13 women, shot arrows through dogs and cats he
trapped as a child. Columbine shooters Eric Harris
and Dylan Klebold boasted about mutilating animals
for fun.

Motivations Behind Animal Cruelty

Most commonly, children who abuse animals have
either witnessed or experienced abuse themselves. For
example, statistics show that 30 percent of children
who have witnessed domestic violence act out a similar
type of violence against their pets. In fact, the link
between animal abuse and interpersonal violence
is so well-known that many U.S. communities now
cross-train social-service and animal-control agencies
in how to recognize signs of animal abuse as possible
indicators of other abusive behaviors.

The "Cry-for-Help" Abuser: (6/7 - 12) This is a
child who intellectually understands that it is not okay
to hurt animals. This behavior is not due to a lack
of education instead, the animal abuse is more likely
to be a symptom of a deeper psychological problem.

As previously noted, a number of studies have linked childhood animal abuse to domestic violence in the home as well as childhood physical or sexual abuse.

Seek professional assistance. I'm a big believer in parents' abilities to weather many of the normal ups and downs of child-rearing without professional assistance, but this is an exception. It is not normal for a child this age to intentionally mistreat an animal.

Clinical Wisdom from Carol Davis, LCSW

> In every difficult situation is potential value.
> Believe this, then begin looking for it.
> —Norman Vincent Peale

As I reviewed this story, I was aware of how overwhelming and humbling it is to be a parent. There is no other job on this planet that comes with no manuals and limited instruction. As parents, we read and consult with family and friends to understand our children as they grow and develop. Once there is a sense that something has gone amiss in your child's development, understanding your child becomes a journey with many pitfalls. Multiple diagnoses and labels may be assigned to your child. If I were a therapist involved with this situation, I would want to explore several topics.

There are moments in every child's life when food becomes an issue. Some children are picky eaters, and some are problem feeders. There is a distinction, and children aren't always ready to eat what adults eat. An alert would go off in my mind that perhaps this child is not being overtly difficult. He could be dealing with a sensory processing disorder (SPD). If that is the case, this child is in need of services to assess his processing issues. Occupational therapy may be needed, and the child might feel misunderstood.

SPD is a neurological disorder comprising of sensory information that a person receives is processed with abnormal responses. A child who does not detect, modulate, and understand sensory input may have atypical responses. Jean Ayres, PhD says SPD is similar to a neurological "traffic jam" that prevents certain parts of the brain from receiving information and interpreting sensory information.

What are the sensory systems? How does this apply to this story? The boy clearly was suffering from SPD. We often take our senses for granted because there is no interference going on. Most of us are free to process and enjoy our families and social situations. For children with SPD, life is hard to navigate because they are dealing with the traffic jam twenty-four hours per day. There are eight sensory systems:

- Visual: difficulty tracking information due to sensitivity to light and possible concentration issues
- Auditory: difficulty interpreting characteristics of sensory stimulation/sensitivity to noise and sounds of everyday life
- Tactile: skin sensitivity to materials, clothing, food, and soaps
- Olfactory: smells are interfered with in processing information
- Gustatory: taste is impaired, and eating issues are prevalent
- Vestibular: movement of the body through space and against gravity
- Proprioception: joint and muscles are affected/relationship to one's own body
- Interceptive: Impulses and nerves are heightened, resulting in behavior issues

There is so much to learn about development, especially when there are delays. The good news that I share with parents is early intervention. With sensory-integration activities, parents can learn from professionals in the field of occupational therapy and speech therapy and enhance a child's future. The challenge is finding the right activities and strategies to assist your child.

I assume that the Wilkes family sought conventional means to handle behavior issues. Understanding a child's behavior and communication at home is key. A child will continue to pull from his environment, albeit in the home or school to express his needs.

When a child exhibits aggression toward animals, something is going wrong in his or her life (possibly within the family). I would hypothesize that this boy witnessed violence toward himself or someone else in the home. The boy is communicating, and no one is listening. A child will hurt an animal to control the environment. If parents witness a child displaying this behavior, it is essential to get professional help. If it is not addressed, it can lead to serious issues. It is entirely possible that given the scope of SPD, the animal could also stimulate processing information to the child that he has difficulty processing.

Blanchard, Kenneth and Johnson, Spencer *The One-Minute Manager,* William Morris & Company, (1982).

Johnston, Joni E, (April 2011) "Children who are cruel to animals: When to worry," *Psychology Today*

Four-Letter Words and a Loogey on the Floor

I don't consider myself a neat freak, but I like a clean house and organization as much as the next guy. I think it comes from my days as a chef. I was taught to clean as I went and proper sanitation methods when handling food. I had to maintain a clean workspace in the kitchen and my tools had to be organized and kept in good working order. Cleanliness, respect for others, and a strong work ethic were always high on my mom's list—and God help you if you talked back.

My mother and father were pretty tough on the four of us. We were not permitted to talk back or be disrespectful. Doing either was signing your own death warrant. They didn't think it was cute. Marty and Eileen didn't think twice about beating their philosophy into you like a Japanese guard from the Omori Prison Camp of 1941.

Their methods were questionable at times. They could have said or done things differently, but I'm glad they were serious about what they expected from their children. I think that's what's missing today. There are parents who think that misbehavior, poor manners, and disrespect from young children is cute. They say, "I don't want to upset him," "He's just so smart," or "He's not challenged enough in school." Does intelligence allow a child to be rude, crude, and disrespectful?

Gabby's mother brought her to the school for discipline and focus. She was very smart, and her mother hoped we could reinforce "that respect thing."

The mother said, "Oh, by the way, she walks around the house saying 'fuck you' all the time." A six-year-old angelic-looking girl said "fuck you" to everyone in the house. The f-bomb was dropped on the mom, the dad, the little brother, the grandma, the grandpa, and even the family dog. She told us this that nugget with a smile and a chuckle.

I didn't care if the kid could split an atom or perform gastric bypass on her mother. I was not impressed and didn't think the mom should be smiling or chuckling. She didn't seem embarrassed or upset.

Master Andrew informed Gabby's mother that language and behavior like that would not be tolerated at the school. The mom thought karate will be great for her princess, and we enrolled Gabby in a basic program. Gabby did well in class and thrived when we encouraged her.

Gabby decided to test the instructors. I guess she thought it would be cute to see what she could get away with. When the instructor turned his back to correct a student, Gabby spat on the floor. It wasn't because she had a terrible cough and was fighting bronchitis. She decided to spit on the floor because it was what she wanted to do.

Master Andrew happened to witness the loogey hitting the floor. He saw her cover it with her foot and rub it into the floor. When Master Andrew asked her to remove her foot, it was clinging to her foot and my floor like a white blood cell clings to an infection.

After reprimanding Gabby and sanitizing the floor, Master Andrew brought Gabby to her mom and said, "I think you need to speak to your daughter about how wrong it is to spit on people's floors."

Gabby sat with her mom for the remainder of the class. After class, Master Andrew walked over to Gabby and her mother.

The mom chuckled and said, "Isn't it amazing what kids will do?"

"No, children will do what they are allowed to do," Master Andrew said.

The mom just laughed it off.

Master Andrew is a father of three and a two-tour war veteran. "Gabby, if you have to spit on the floor, do it when you go home—not here." He turned to the mother. "What would you do if she did that at home?"

"She does do it at home, and she gets in trouble for it."

Gabby was not getting the correction she desperately needed. If poor behavior and disrespect are tolerated at home, children will do it outside the home as well.

Gabby and her mom didn't go back to class for two weeks. The mom told Master Andrew that she had a talk with Gabby and promised that it wouldn't happen again. She also mentioned that Gabby wrote an apology card, which they left at home. Gabby and her mother came to one more class after that, and we never saw or heard from them again.

Poor behavior, disrespect, a foul mouth, and disregard for people and their property will never be embraced by anyone. I hope Gabby and mom get their arms around this concept before it's too late. Clinical Wisdom from Carol Davis, LCSW

> You have to do your own growing no matter
> how tall your grandfather was.
> —Abraham Lincoln

Children need real heroes to emulate. Today's culture is running the risk of raising entitled children who live lives of failure and disappointment. Typically, a parent enrolls a child in karate school to develop moral character, discipline, and mental focus.

The tenets of a black belt are something for young people to aspire to: honesty, integrity, respect, perseverance, and an indomitable spirit. In this scenario, we see the intention was there for Gabby to use respectful language and improve her behavior. Schools and outside activities can enhance a child's life, but they cannot replace the lessons that need to be taught at home. It requires a firm foundation to become good citizens who are capable of enduring and enjoying life. This is often easier said than done, and it often feels daunting and impossible.

Teaching values takes time, which has become a scarce commodity due to the demands on parents to make ends meet. Parents are exhausted, and children are influenced by television, video games, and the Internet. Growing up in this fast-paced world is a tall order, and we need to take the time to nourish our children's minds and bodies by dedicating parent-child time as an activity. It is accessible and does not cost money.

The art of storytelling is getting lost in our culture. I suggest parents spend quality time with their children by telling them stories about prominent family members or other heroes from history. Children gravitate toward superheroes as they grow. Genuine heroes can teach respect and values to children. Telling stories about heroes can be useful. It teaches them about genuineness, self-sacrificing behaviors, and values. Additionally, it allows for time together in a nourishing activity.

I know this child is headed for problems because she has not learned respect, integrity, honesty, and perseverance. As a result, her spirit is wounded—and she will have struggles in life. Karate could help!

If I could intervene with this family, I would listen for the parents' story to see if I could understand their acceptance of disrespect. I would encourage change to begin within the family and continue in the social world. Someone needs to talk with the mom and dad to discover why this behavior is acceptable. The parents may have suffered and are passing on their stories to Gabby.

Storytelling in therapy is an effective way to understand problems. We all have stories that need to be told and understood. Unfortunately, we don't know enough about this family's story. I hope Gabby will change her behavior.

Grandma needs a slap.

> The times they are a-changing.
> —Bob Dylan.

More and more grandparents are raising children these days. Many grandparents have taken over the roles of the parents. The children they raised have failed. Some have failed miserably at the most important job they would ever hold: being a loving, responsible parent.

Thank god for grandparents. Phyllis was rough around the edges. She looked much older than her years. The first time I met Phyllis, she was a mess. She looked like she had just rolled out of bed. She had unkempt hair, no makeup, dirty sweatpants, and a stained Budweiser T-shirt at five o'clock on a Wednesday.

She brought her two grandsons for an introductory appointment, and we welcomed them with our usual smiles. Master Dave did the initial personal analysis. He asked about the children's needs and what benefits the family was looking for (focus, confidence, self-defense skills, etc.).

Master Dave asked, "So, why martial arts for your grandson?"

"Look at him. He's fat!" the grandma said in front of Dylan.

Dylan was obviously embarrassed.

Master Dave pretended he didn't hear what grandma said and proceeded to the next question. "Will Mom and Dad be joining us today?"

"No. Mom's a loser, and Dad's in jail for drugs."

She had no filter, no class, and no clue. I'm sure she was just tired and mentally exhausted from the day-to-day grind of raising two small boys and having to live a life she probably wasn't prepared for. We gave her the benefit of the doubt and proceeded to the lesson. The kids did great. They responded to Master Dave, and we signed them up.

Grandma was a drop-and-go parent. She brought them to class late, brought them to the wrong class, or picked them up late. I wondered if it made her boys feel unimportant? Could it make them feel like their grandma didn't care?

The grandma had a lot to say when she did come into the school. In the presence of her grandsons, she said, "He's not getting any better. He's lazy." She had a habit of comparing the children, but they were making good progress. They went from being shy and aloof to gaining confidence and trusting the staff.

Master Dave said, "The boys are doing well and making progress."

"Really? From here, it looks like they don't know shit."

Children need correction. Children need rules and boundaries. Children need to feel safe and loved. She knew what the boys had gone through with absent parents and shuffling between homes and family members. Why wasn't she protecting these boys and showering them with praise and encouragement?

Another day, Grandma said, "Why isn't Dylan confident?"

I wanted to say, "You tell him he's fat, and you tell him he can't do it."

Master Dave said, "Of course he lacks confidence. Build him up—don't tear him down."

Grandma looked at us and smirked.

I told her that a positive something is better than a negative anything. "And if you feel you need to say something to the boys, please correct them in private—and praise them publicly."

I will never understand people who are comfortable with saying anything and everything. Those poor souls feel it is their mission in life to point out the flaws and imperfections of others—like there is a reward for it. They need to criticize, condemn, and correct with contempt. Let us be encouragers. Let us be the finders of gold within all of us. The world has enough critics. Children need encouragement, praise, correction, and love.

I'm sure she was just repeating what she had been subjected to. The past does not equal the future. I hope she stops repeating what she knows about parenting and starts being an encourager. I hope she turns into a finder of gold instead of a digger of dirt.

Clinical Wisdom from Carol Davis, LCSW

> Catch people doing something right.
> —Ken Blanchard, PhD, and Spencer Johnson,
> MD, The One-Minute Manager

Constant criticism is a form of child abuse. Children who are frequently criticized learn to doubt themselves and form belief systems that leave them helpless with low levels of confidence and self-worth. It can lead to self-sabotaging behaviors and limit success. Children view their parents and caregivers as all-knowing and internalize their words as truth.

Many parents think they are teaching their children by pointing out their faults. Criticism demotivates and discourages children. It squashes any instinct to take risks and try new adventures. Alienation and withdrawal lead to depression. The criticism gets stored in the body. Children will remember if they are called stupid or lazy. It becomes a self-fulfilling prophecy, and it is a difficult cycle to deal with as young adults and older adults attempt to disbelieve ingrained belief systems.

The grandma was creating a cycle of emotional abuse that could take years to untangle. Words of encouragement, appreciation, and support are crucial in the development of healthy self-esteem. Stephanie Marston, child psychotherapist and author of The Magic of

Encouragement, confirms in her research at the University of Calgary the damage verbal abuse does to children is profound and lasting. Her book offers specific tools for coping with frustrating behaviors. She encourages parents to learn skills to enhance children's self-esteem. The skills involved are encouraging cooperation, avoiding daily power struggles, saying no, encouraging children to express feelings, helping parents express anger constructively and bypass negative criticism, and setting clear and firm limits while encouraging independence and responsibility. The overall goal is to help parents develop competence and confidence in their children while improving communication and breaking self-destructive family patterns.

The One-Minute Manager reveals a secret for managers by reinforcing the huge benefits that occur when someone notices a person doing something right. Being a parent is very similar to being a manager. The difference is there are no promotions or advances in your career. I like this quote because of its simplicity. Being a parent is not simple, but there are solutions to problems with children. It is possible to overcome the ill effects of negative criticism with help. As human beings, we want to be recognized and valued—and children need that in order to develop into healthy adults.

Children require praise and approval. I encourage parents to spend time—even ten minutes per day—with their children by actively listening to their days or their problems. If there are no problems, perhaps there are humorous events worth sharing. Patience and encouragement are valuable tools in parenting, and I acknowledge the stress and difficulty parents experience. However, there is nothing more valuable than taking the time to listen. The rewards will continue for years to come! Children value your time—even if it is a small amount. It teaches them that they matter, and that lesson remains with them for a lifetime.

Another valuable solution to difficult situations with children is modeling apologies. This does not excuse misbehavior or diminish your authority as a parent. When a parent apologizes, the parent is modeling a crucial lesson in interpersonal relationships. The parent gains authority with the child because children internalize an adult's authority based on respect.

If warranted, apologies are a gift. They acknowledge our humanity and tend to soften situations when tender feelings are exchanged.

5

Self-Control

You have power over your mind—not outside events.
Realize this, and you will find strength.
—Marcus Aurelius

Broken Trophy

Competition is a good thing, and it brings out the best in us. It pushes students, children, and competitors to new heights. It forces us to break through the chains of mediocrity and comfort. The only problem I see with competition is that the best person doesn't always win, but that can be a great thing too. For some reason, parents want to insulate children from the pangs of defeat. Why? Isn't there a life lesson there somewhere? Can't we learn from our mistakes? In the martial arts, which I feel should be a subject in American physical education classes, people say, "A black belt is a white belt who didn't quit."

We don't quit or give up. As martial artists or "karate-ka's, we fully understand that defeat and setbacks occur in training. There is no honor in giving up or stopping. There is no honor in complaining. To complain or whine is to give life to it. There is no honor or good in that. Honor is a word that needs to make a drastic and quick comeback in our society.

"Failure is the mother of success." I love this Chinese saying. Any failure I have had has propelled me to learn from it and use it as a stepping-stone to achieve my goals. Parents are blueprints for their children. Children take their cues from parental examples.

Bad examples show up on baseball, soccer, and football fields, in dance competitions, cheer, gymnastics, and other organized sports, and in recreation programs for kids, parents, and coaches.

We had a tournament that started in the morning. There were hundreds of competitors. The divisions were broken down by age and rank, and there were categories like Kata, weapons, sparring, and even an open division. Tournaments are long and slow. The parents are anxious for their children, and the children are anxious to perform and compete. Instructors and referees are trying their best to expedite all the competitors in a timely fashion so parents and families can receive a fair and pleasant day of judging. Sometimes things don't go as planned.

The tournament was winding down, and some black belts were starting to clean up, empty garbage, and dismantle equipment. Some divisions were still active, including the brown and black belts. After several hours of judging and barking commands, I relished the idea of sitting quietly.

Two parents walked up and told me what a great experience it was for their child. They were impressed with how professional and organized the tournament was. They showered me with praise and compliments, which really made my day. As this was going on, I noticed one of the dads from another school walking toward a garbage can. I'm pretty good at reading people and body language. He was walking at a fast pace with strong posture, and he never took his eyes off of me. He was obviously agitated about something. After a few seconds of direct eye contact, he stopped at the garbage can, held up his son's trophy, and broke it in half. He threw it away in front of his son!

I excused myself and decided to confront the father. I thought it was strange because I'd had no dealings with the man or his son. I did not grade or judge the boy. He was not in any groups I judged or refereed.

I approached him with a smile and said, "Are you okay? Is there something I can help you with? You seem angry."

His twelve-year-old son was crying.

I said, "Are you guys okay? You threw away your trophy? Why?"

The father said, "It's third place. It should've been first."

I was blown away. He threw his son's trophy away because it was for third place? I wonder if he ever won anything himself? Did he ever compete? I felt such anger for this fool and such sadness for his son. What parent does this? I said, "First or third place makes no difference. Your son competed, and he should be praised for what he did."

He turned his back on me and walked away.

My instructor happened to witness it. He approached the parent and chastised him for his behavior and conduct. I believe he was later kicked out of his school and forbidden to attend any school events in the future.

The child was collateral damage of his father's poor behavior. I guess he thought he was teaching his child a lesson. What could the lesson be? Do not settle for less than best? Third place is no place? I can't imagine the embarrassment his son felt. The life lesson is one I'm sure the boy will repeat—unless he is mentally strong enough to realize he must not follow in his dad's footsteps.

Here's a great poem that helps us all remember:

The Little Chap Who Follows Me!

A careful man I want to be;
A little fellow follows me.
I do not dare to go astray
For fear he'll go the self same way.
I cannot once escape his eyes,

Whate'er he sees me do, he tries.
Like me he says he's going to be;
The little chap who follows me.

Clinical Wisdom from Carol Davis, LCSW

Nothing is to be clung to as I, me, or mine." In other
words, no attachments—especially to fixed
ideas of yourself and who you are.
—Jon Kabat-Zinn

Jon Kabat-Zinn is a well-known professor of medicine at the University
of Massachusetts Medical School. He created the Stress Reduction
Clinic and the Center for Mindfulness. His greatest contribution was
integrating mindfulness, which helps people cope with stress, anxiety,
pain, and illness with medicine. He started the clinic in 1979—
before yoga and meditation emerged in the West. He recognized
that one could become so attached to an idea about pain, illness, or
competition that the attachment to the thought could interfere with
the outcome. Parents can become so involved in their children's lives
and achievements that it is possible to lose sight of their needs. In this
situation, the father was so attached to winning first place that he
negated his child's efforts and achievements.

A plethora of issues are present in this scenario. My main concerns
would be the child's self-worth and the impact on his life. Who is this
child? What message is he going home with? There was no failure
to learn from, but the father displayed anger and shame. The pain
associated with low self-worth and parental disapproval can result in
years of therapy as an adult.

Our children are not our property or a fulfillment of our trials.
This child could develop anxiety and depression from repeated
incidents with his father. It's important to know who your children
are and celebrate their uniqueness—not our versions of who they are.

As a parent, it is crucial to be mindful and aware of your unresolved issues and seek help for them if necessary.

Your wife peed her pants.

There are certain things you don't learn in school or college. I'm a very patient guy, and that patience has served me well as a martial arts instructor. My instructor, Grand Master Art Beins, passed on many gifts to me, but one of the greatest gifts was a saying: "Always make a never-ending correction with a smile." That gem reminds us to correct students with a smile—no matter how many times it takes the student to learn a technique. Never let a student know you may be losing patience. I use this technique when I deal with frustrating, anxious, overbearing, or rude parents.

Like most days, we were busy at the school. Classes were packed, which made me happy. The instructors were working their plans, the kids were energetic and working hard, and I had time to get some bookwork done. I did payroll, paid some bills, and did some marketing to promote the school before my next class.

As I worked diligently, there was a gentle knock on my door. I looked up and saw a mother of one of the children in the class. She was a low-maintenance, pro-school client. She said, "Do you have a minute?"

"Of course. How can I help you?"

"I think you need to come up front. There's a mother up there who peed her pants."

It was four o'clock in the afternoon! I thanked her for bringing it to my attention, and I took a minute to think about what I was going to say.

The lobby was full of parents, and a lady was leaning against the receptionist's desk. She was soaked in urine from her hips to her ankles. Did she have a burst catheter or a bladder problem? Why is she standing there? Why isn't she running for the bathroom? Why isn't she running out of the building? Maybe she can't feel the urine-soaked mom jeans clinging to her legs?

I slowly approached her and said, "How are you?"

She said, "Fine. How are you?"

I could smell the alcohol on her breath. She was so loaded that she had pissed her pants and didn't know it. I smiled and walked back to my office to call her husband. I thought it would be best for her not to drive herself or her son home.

The husband answered the phone and said, "What did she do?"

"I think you need to come pick your wife up."

"Okay. What did she do?"

"She peed her pants, and I think she might have had too much to drink today."

He sighed in disgust and told me that her drinking had gotten out hand. It had been going on for years, and he was done.

I had no experience with that sort of thing, but I said, "I'm sorry for what you're going through. From one husband and father to another, she is jeopardizing her own safety, her son's, and others."

When he picked her up, she gave him a hug and asked him what he was doing there.

He made up an excuse, and they all went home. The other parents about what had happened. "How could a mother do that?" "She drove her kid drunk?" "She peed herself and didn't know it!"

The weeks that followed were uneventful. I thought all was wonderful—until a mother informed me that the lady was trying to back up in the parking lot. She kept backing out, pulling in, backing out, and pulling back in.

She had also called the cops. Something needed to wake her up—better a cop than an accident with her child in the car or injuring another person.

The cops questioned her and gave her a sobriety test. I assume she passed because they let her go.

How could that be?

Not long after that, I received a call from the lady. "Why did you call the fucking police on me?"

"I didn't call the cops, but I wish I did. I should've called them last week when you peed all over yourself. Remember that?"

She hung up on me, and she never set foot in the school again. Her husband took the son to classes for about a month after that, and then he filed for divorce. I never saw them again. I hope she got help for her drinking and the child was not affected by the mother's careless and selfish ways.

According to the American Academy of Child and Adolescent Psychiatry, a child being raised by a parent or caregiver who is suffering from alcohol abuse may have a variety of conflicting emotions that need to be addressed in order to avoid future problems. They are in a difficult position because they cannot go to their own parents for support. Some of the feelings can include the following:

- Guilt. The child may see himself or herself as the main cause of the mother's or father's drinking.
- Anxiety. The child may worry constantly about the situation at home. He or she may fear the alcoholic parent will become sick or injured and may fear fights and violence between the parents.
- Embarrassment. Parents may give the child the message that there is a terrible secret at home. The ashamed child does not invite friends home and is afraid to ask anyone for help.
- Inability to have close relationships. Because the child has been disappointed by the drinking parent many times, he or she often does not trust others.
- Confusion. The alcoholic parent will change suddenly from being loving to angry, regardless of the child's behavior. A regular daily schedule, which is very important for a child, does not exist because bedtimes and mealtimes are constantly changing.

- Anger. The child feels anger at the alcoholic parent for drinking, and may be angry with the nonalcoholic parent for lack of support and protection.
- Depression. The child feels lonely and helpless to change the situation.

Although the child tries to keep the alcoholism a secret, teachers, relatives, other adults, or friends may sense that something is wrong. Teachers and caregivers should be aware that the following behaviors may signal a drinking or other problem at home:

- failure in school, truancy
- lack of friends, withdrawal from classmates
- delinquent behavior, such as stealing or violence
- frequent physical complaints, such as headaches or stomachaches
- abuse of drugs or alcohol
- aggression toward other children
- risky behaviors
- depression or suicidal thoughts or behavior

I'm a firm believer that parents, guardians, leaders, bosses, instructors, teachers, coaches, and people in positions of influence have a solemn duty to set examples. Our history and our past do not equal our future—or our children's futures. We should be mindful and present enough not to pass our deficiencies on to our children.

Clinical Wisdom from Carol Davis, LCSW

Coincidence is God's way of remaining anonymous.
—Albert Einstein

In my many years of clinical practice, I have encountered this scenario in many different settings, and it leaves a pit in my stomach. The child does not understand the alcoholic behavior and is at risk for a multitude of emotional traumas. Often, people unknowingly participate in the denial system by looking the other way and not addressing the situation.

Alcoholism is accompanied by vast amounts of denial (as illustrated in this story). A mother can urinate in a public place, deny there is any reason to be concerned, and have no understanding of the danger of driving while impaired. Albert Einstein's words remind me of the long and winding road of addiction. A situation like this can be the start of a seed or a coincidence.

Claudia Black, author of *It Will Never Happen to Me*, informed us of the many risks for children in alcoholic homes. These children are at risk of remaining in an alcoholic system or developing alcoholism themselves. They learn three rules that can affect children in social, educational, and familial relationships.

- Don't talk about the real issue.
- Don't trust.
- Don't feel.

The incident at the karate school could be the start of healing for the child. Healing occurs in many stages for children from alcoholic homes. It could be helpful to a child who might experience isolation, embarrassment, and shame on a regular basis. The silence is cracked, and caring adults are now aware of the situation.

The rules in the child's can start to unravel. Someone in the school could begin to talk to the child and develop a trusting relationship. Denial and delusion are present in alcoholic families. In psychiatry, delusions are defined as a fixed belief that is resistant to reason or confrontation with actual facts (Dictionary.com).

In alcoholism, there are beliefs that are accepted by the alcoholics and the family systems. Often, the beliefs become fixed in families and have stifling effects on the children. Spouses and children accept the reality of the alcoholic's behavior as normal in order to maintain balance in the family system. Healing and recovery happen when the two defenses are challenged and new pathways open for the families.

Black, Claudia, *It Will Never Happen to Me*, Hazelden Publishing, (2002).

Biker Boy

I was trying to come up with an awesome, exciting ad that would bring droves of students to my school. Outside, the parents were chatty— and the instructors had built great energy in class by adding music. The students were excited, and I could almost feel the class coming through the walls.

Dawn ran down hallway of the school and commanded me to "get my ass up to the front." Two knucklehead fathers were fighting in my lobby. I could hear them bouncing off my walls while their kids were taking karate class. I ran up to the front, and two fathers were hitting each other and locked in a clinch. Four or five mothers were protecting their kids.

One of the fighters was a biker guy would come into the school in leather dirty jeans with a chain for his wallet and a bandanna around his head. I don't even know if he owned a motorcycle. Maybe he owned a Schwinn, but I never saw the bike. He was always a problem. Nothing was ever good enough for him. He'd bring a small boy to class, and his even younger boy would cause havoc in the lobby. He would punch and kick and spit on the other little kids. He would take their toys and break them. There was never any correction from the biker dad.

The other father was a small-framed, well-groomed man who looked like an accountant. The accountant was doing the beating of the biker dad. I got between the two fathers. I had biker boy by the face, pushed him against the front desk, and kicked the other father in the chest.

The class stopped. The kids wanted to see what was going on, and the mothers in the lobby were in shock.

I walked biker boy out to the parking lot, went back into the school, and walked the other father to my office. I asked, "What the hell is going on? Why in God's name would you attack this man in front of your own children?"

"He's been sleeping with my wife. He's been having an affair with my wife."

I should have been upset, but I felt unbelievably sad for him. I reprimanded him and told him how wrong he was and how disrespectful he was to me and the school, but if I knew that was the case, I would've taken my time going up to the front. I would have let the accountant guy tee off on the biker a little bit more.

Two days later, the biker came back with his two sons. He tried not to make eye contact with me.

I approached him and said, "That was wrong on so many levels— and it will never happen again."

As I finished my sentence, the younger son punched me in the groin.

I said, "And another thing, keep this kid under control. He disturbs the class. He disturbs the peace out here with the other children. Keep him under control."

The biker said, "I'll take care of it, but you show me some respect."

Respect? Did this guy just tell me to show him some respect? He must have been high.

"Sure," I said. "I'd be glad to show you some respect. If you follow me to my office, I will give you all the respect you can handle!"

He did not follow me back to the office. I guess he did not want any of my respect. I was not going to give him respect. I was going to give him the benefit of my many years of martial art training. It would have been a great private lesson. I was younger when that happened—and probably not as patient as I am now.

The following week, I received an anonymous letter from one of the mothers. It said how unprofessional I was in handling the biker. Deep down, he was really a nice guy, a good father, and a good provider. I shouldn't have been so hard on him. She was disappointed in me.

What kind of person does this? What message does this send to her children?

I understand there are many unhappy people out there, and many of them are married. Infidelity, lies, cheating, and public violence are not welcome in my backyard!

We expect so much from our children. We want academic achievers, varsity athletes with promise of scholarships, leaders, and well-behaved, mannerly, and respectful children. Where does it come from? The parents.

If grown adults can act like that in a public place surrounded by other adults and children, what goes on in the privacy of their own homes? What goes on among the comfortable surroundings of friends and family?

Clinical Wisdom from Carol Davis, LCSW

> Home is that youthful place where a child is the only real living inhabitant. Parents, siblings, and neighbors are mysterious apparitions who come, go and do strange unfathomable things in and around the child, the region's only enfranchised citizen.
> —Maya Angelou, Letter to my Daughter

Children are so dependent on the folks they are born to and live with. They learn how to relate, love, hate, fight, play, and dream about their futures within the confines of their homes. Today's children are faced with the challenges of technology and isolation due to the demands on parents and the schedules they maintain. There is pressure to perform in sports, school, and extracurricular activities. Children are encouraged to succeed and plan for their futures before they reach the developmental stage needed to achieve mental health.

The American Psychological Association published a report based on a study. In "Stress in America," Millennials were rated as the most stressed. The study looked at stress among generations. Millennials reported high levels of stress in sleep disturbance, increased irritability, anger, depression, and anxiety.

Children who are exposed to violence often suffer from despair, which may manifest as physical symptoms like headaches, stomachaches, bowel problems, cold sores, and bed-wetting. It may be difficult for children to focus due to anxiety and their short attention spans.

In this situation, the children were trained in martial arts to contain mental anguish. How confusing to have parents engaging in a public fight! There was confusion for the children about the nature of the fight. I have seen many parents outraged at bullying in school, but they do not recognize the bullying they sometimes model for their children. Children absorb these encounters and internalize the lessons from their parents. In this case, the child might learn to endorse violence and insecurity. How can a child make sense of two fathers fighting in this manner? We need to be mindful that our children are learning all the time from parents.

Maya Angelou writes about the importance of a home and how folks travel through life with home as the guiding post. Parents have a responsibility to instill values that can help children cope with life's complexities. In my years of clinical practice, I have seen many situations where children develop anxiety and depressive disorders from early experiences that were incomprehensible to them.

6

Courtesy

He who sows courtesy reaps friendship, and
he who plants kindness gathers love.
—Saint Basil

Please and thank you are still magic words.

It's my guess that no parents think they're bad parents when they are parenting. This observation comes from seeing the culmination of their failures in their grown children. If we went into our memory banks and sought out the answers we were looking for, we might find that we didn't enforce household rules and boundaries on a consistent basis.

What are the household rules and boundaries? In my house growing up, my parents had many rules:

+ Put the toilet seat down.
+ Don't raise your voice.
+ If you make a mess, clean it up.
+ Say please, thank you, and excuse me.
+ No calls during dinner hour.
+ Watch your language.

One time, I felt like I had to debate my mother about something. I must have been feeling my oats. I continued to harass my mother about whatever it was, and she began to scream at me.

My father and his hot Irish temper walked into that verbal thrashing.

I attempted to inform my father about why I was arguing and raising my voice to my mother. I said, "She's not listening to me."

The vein in his temple began to enlarge, and he made me repeat what I had said.

I knew I had stepped on a landmine, but I was fifteen and knew everything. I said, "She's not listening to me."

"She? Who's she?"

"Mom," I said.

"That's my wife—and your mother!"

I felt like a ton bricks had fallen on my head. He was loud, intimidating, forceful, direct, and never to be forgotten.

And there it was in a nutshell. I broke a household rule and boundary. I raised my voice to my mother. There was no worrying about my feelings or my situation. Marty came down hard and loud so I wouldn't forget it. I never did forget it.

There was an immediate and direct response for breaking the rules. My parents didn't wait to speak with me. They didn't request a meeting three days later with my instructor or guidance counselor to talk about my poor behavior. They dealt with it swiftly. They were swift and consistent. If one of us broke a rule or disrespected the other, it was game on.

It was real. It was old-school parenting. With my staff, I call it PCP (praise-correct-praise). It works well with parenting and extremely well with teaching: one minute of praise, one minute of correction, and one more minute of praise.

In my parents' case, the correcting part normally went on longer than a minute—and they fell short with dishing out the praise—but they never made excuses for their children's poor behavior or lack of manners.

Parents who fall short in the parenting department have one distinguishable trait in common: They know all the reasons for their failure to correct the child. They have excuses and alibis for their children. They have what they believe is an airtight alibi to explain their own lack of parental consistency.

Some of these excuses are clever, and some are justifiable. In more than thirty-five years of working with children and their parents, I have heard a gaggle of alibis from parents. Some of the most commonly used excuses are as follows:

- He's just being a kid.
- He's only _____ years old.
- He's tired.
- He's not being challenged enough.
- He's bored.
- He's just so smart.
- He's shy.
- It's his father's fault.
- It's his mother's fault.
- He has a lot of energy.
- I'm tired.
- I have to pick my battles.
- He's high-spirited.
- He's very emotional.
- I get no support.
- I'm tired of fighting with him.
- I don't want to upset him.
- That's how he expresses himself.
- He's just being a boy.
- He just woke up from his nap.
- He just got home from …

- o Grandma's
- o Grandpa's
- o Aunt/Uncle's
- o summer camp
- o a friend's house
- o the beach
- o the swimming pool
- He's just so cute.
- He's just so adorable.

I have heard those alibis and excuses from parents too many times to count. Parents seem to hold on to these excuses for their children's poor behavior. Why? I think it's obvious. They created the excuse, and now they must defend it. The moms and dads have consented to the behavior that they seem to be having trouble with. Why not correct the problem or flaw?

When parents ask for an office chat or want to speak about poor behavior at home, I ask a series of questions:

- Why is this allowed?
- Why are you tolerating this?
- Why is this consistently happening?
- Why do feel you can't correct this?

The parents usually refer to the list of alibis. In the karate school, my instructors have a creed we live by.

The Instructor's Creed

- I am patient and enthusiastic.
- I lead by example.
- I will teach each class as if it is the most important class I will ever teach.

Maybe we should change it to the Parent Creed.

- ☐ I am my child's example.
- ☐ I will be patient, consistent, and enthusiastic.
- ☐ I will plant the seeds of greatness into my child because I know there is nothing more important.

Children need to be corrected many, many times, and the fruits of the discipline and PCP style often won't ripen until the children are grown. If we don't sow the seeds of greatness into our children today, we cannot expect to reap them tomorrow.

Clinical Wisdom from Carol Davis, LCSW

As a therapist, I like the concept of praise-correct-praise used by Master Paul and his instructors. It is based in positive psychology, and it is a lifelong practice that is needed when raising children. Children require direction and correction, which can be tireless for parents. It has tremendous benefits of children. They internalize the seeds that were planted by parents and teachers as they enter adulthood. Martial arts utilizes repetition to learn the art of karate, and mastering it requires time and patience.

Raising children to be strong and healthy requires repetition. The results of the discipline and correction often are not recognized until adulthood. I encourage parents to obtain emotional support wherever they can in order to master the art of parenting. The PCP style utilized at the school and patience with disciplining your children will ripen because children require repetition to learn life's lessons.

7

Six Degrees of Awesome

> We are what we repeatedly do.
> —Aristotle

Being a parent is a tough job. At times, it seems like a thankless job. It comes with no handbook, no service contract, and no formal instruction. It requires constant on-the-job training, but the payoff is pure joy, love, respect, admiration, and honor.

It is an honor to be blessed with a child and have the privilege of cultivating these beautiful souls into positive, productive people.

There's a cute story about two men at a business seminar in Texas. One man was highly successful, dressed well, spoke well, and was worth several million dollars. The other man was new to business, and he was very eager to learn the secrets of the successful man.

After several minutes of chatting, the second man said, "So, what's your secret? How'd you get so rich?"

The successful Texan said, "How did I get so rich? It's easy, son. You find out what the poor people are doing—and you don't do that!"

Model your behaviors on those you wish to be like. Read their books, speak like they speak, act like they act, visit the places they visit, and educate yourself and train as they do. Do what the successful parent does.

Being a positive example is one way to master successful parenting. Each chapter of this book has a principle of black belt excellence. Developing a rock-solid, awesome kid requires the six principles of a black belt. We call them the six degrees of awesomeness. To avoid falling short in our roles as parents, six degrees must be incorporated and practiced:

- perseverance
- honesty
- integrity
- courtesy
- self-control
- respect

We teach these principles to our children through our examples.

Perseverance is the ability to continue despite difficulty and adversity. Our children should know the stories of our family heritage and how our parents and grandparents struggled and continued onward and upward—never giving up on the quest for greatness and success. If you don't have a family heritage that is rich in stories of perseverance, then history is filled with stories of great people overcoming adversity. Read to your children and fill their minds with positive, enriching stories.

Honesty is simple and straightforward, but it is not so easy for some people. Martial artists are taught the value of honor and respect from the first time we step on the mats in the dojo. There is no honor in using the power of our techniques to hurt or bully others.

Years ago, I went to a seminar with Grand Master Jhoon Rhee, the father of American Tae Kwon Do:

> When you are truthful, you are beautiful in the heart. When you are beautiful in the heart, everybody loves you. When everybody loves you, you are happy.

On the other hand, when you lie, you become ugly in the heart. When you are ugly in the heart, everybody hates you. When everybody hates you, there's no way you can lead a happy life.

When children feel safe and secure and trust their parents, teachers, and friends, they demonstrate honesty. Make children feel safe.

Integrity is doing the right thing even when no one is watching. Integrity walks hand in hand with honesty. The principles families and parents live by could never be tarnished for the sake of easy gain or riches. Teach your children that you are a principled person.

Courtesy: *polite behavior that shows respect for other people.* In Japan, the train system is an example of precision. The trains run like clockwork. If the train is late by as much as a minute, an apology is transmitted to the patrons. If the train is late by fifteen minutes, the conductor walks up and down the car, apologizing to each rider for the inconvenience. A certificate of delay is given to riders so they can give to their employers if they need to. This is the ultimate in courtesy and integrity. Everyone likes a well-mannered child. Our children are a reflection of their parents. Use words like please, hello, thank you, and excuse me. Look others in the eye when speaking. These courtesies are the foundation of respect, and they must be practiced daily and often. Never forget them or let them be watered down.

Self-control: *restraint exercised over one's own impulses, emotions, or desires.* It's tough to ask a child to have self-control when they see us

+ flipping off other drivers,
+ losing of patience because the "line is too long,"
+ needing a cigarette, or
+ needing a drink.

Demonstrating self-control to our children isn't easy, especially if we have been working all day, are sick, or feel stressed. Our children are worth it. Try harder. They are watching you and modeling you.

Respect: *a feeling of admiring someone or something that is good, valuable, important, etc.* We are all entitled to it—from a janitor to the president. Some make it harder for us to show it, but that's on them. Martial arts starts with respect and ends with respect. Respect your husband, wife, partner, brother, sister, teachers, family, and friends. Most important, be sure your children see you and hear you demonstrating that love and respect. They will copy and model what you do.

One of the best ways to ensure that your children grow up with a healthy sense of self-esteem is to show them that their decisions and actions consistently make a difference. How can you do that? Tony Robbins says, "Demonstrate what's possible by being an example."

In parting, I would like thank you for allowing me to share parts of my life and my stories. If you reflect on these stories and strategies and apply them to your life, we will both be luckier.

Success is no accident in a business, a relationship, grades on a report card, or a happy, healthy, productive child.

How do you want to be remembered? As a giant among men? As a hot-tempered father who couldn't tell his wife and kids what they meant to him? As a parent who was too busy to play ball with his kids? On your deathbed, you won't say, "If only I worked twenty more hours of overtime." Leave a lasting legacy. Rear your children so that they are awesome in the six principles: perseverance, integrity, honesty, courtesy, respect, and self-control.

Many years ago, I studied the art of ninjutsu. In one class, the instructor said, "I'm not teaching you how to fight. I'm teaching you how to control evil. That's what we are all doing here." I understand now that he meant we could control the evils of the following:

- ill health
- fear and worry
- indecision and doubt
- greed
- jealously
- anger
- hatred
- physical evils

Stop painful parenting. Be an example of what a strong, consistent, and loving parent should be.

I know you can do it.

Each one—teach one!

Paul Prendergast is a 6th-Degree Black Belt and Master Instructor. He has over 35 years of Martial Arts Experience. For the past 25 years, Master Paul owns and operates two of the most trusted and respected Martial Arts schools in the nation. Master Paul Prendergast teaches an eclectic system of Martial Arts, with an emphasis on Character Development as well as Self Defense. The base of his award winning curriculum is in the art of Kenpo Karate, Jujitsu, and Submission Grappling. Master Paul has taught Self-Defense and tactics to thousands of people including, US National Soccer Team, State and Local Law Enforcement, NJ Board of Realtors, Boy Scouts of America, Girl Scouts, Toms River New Jersey Public Schools K thru 8th grade, and multiple Rape Prevention and Self-defense clinics to various Organizations. He currently owns and operates two schools in New Jersey, where over 500 families attend.

Carol Davis has provided dynamic and empathetic psychotherapy for the past 35 years in Highland Park, Eatontown, NJ and Staten Island NY. Her treatment approach includes an understanding of the individual from a humanistic approach recognizing that each person has a unique experience that shapes an individual's life. Carol's approach encompasses listening for the "life story" and helping individuals and families reach self-acceptance in order to change and grow. Included in her scope is her extensive experience with severe psychological trauma, grief, eating disorders, sexual abuse and all aspects of substance abuse including the impact of these issues on family life.